HUMAN NATURE AND THE HUMAN CONDITION

BOOKS BY JOSEPH WOOD KRUTCH

COMEDY AND CONSCIENCE AFTER THE RESTORATION

EDGAR ALLAN POE—A STUDY IN GENIUS

THE MODERN TEMPER

FIVE MASTERS

EXPERIENCE AND ART

WAS EUROPE A SUCCESS?

THE AMERICAN DRAMA SINCE 1918

SAMUEL JOHNSON

HENRY DAVID THOREAU

THE TWELVE SEASONS

THE DESERT YEAR

THE BEST OF TWO WORLDS

THE VOICE OF THE DESERT

MODERNISM IN MODERN DRAMA

THE MEASURE OF MAN

THE GREAT CHAIN OF LIFE

GRAND CANYON

HUMAN NATURE AND THE HUMAN CONDITION

HUMAN NATURE AND

THE HUMAN CONDITION

by Joseph Wood Krutch

RANDOM HOUSE
New York

Second Printing

© Copyright, 1959, by Joseph Wood Krutch

All rights reserved under International and Pan-American Copyright
Conventions. Published in New York by Random House, Inc., and
simultaneously in Toronto, Canada, by Random House of Canada, Limited.

Library of Congress Catalog Card Number: 59–10808

Design: James McCrea

Manufactured in the United States of America

To Kenneth Bechtel, who introduced me to
some new country both geographical and spiritual

Acknowledgments

Some parts of this book have appeared in different form in the *American Scholar*, and a part of Chapter I appeared in the *Saturday Review*. The author wishes to thank the editors of these magazines for their permission to reprint this material. Other portions of the book were delivered as the Raymond Fred West Memorial Lectures at Stanford University in 1958.

The author also wishes to acknowledge, with thanks, permission to use brief quotations from the following:

The Next Million Years, by Sir Charles Galton Darwin. Copyright 1952 by Charles Galton Darwin. Reprinted by permission of Doubleday & Co., Inc. (copyright holders for the United States and the Philippines), and Rupert Hart-Davis Ltd. (copyright holders for the British Empire).

"High Living Standard Waits," by Elmer Roessner, which appeared in the *Winston-Salem Journal*.

Advantage Points (August, 1954, and February, 1956, issues).

Contents

HUMAN NATURE AND THE HUMAN CONDITION

· I ·

The Twentieth Century: Dawn or Twilight?

In many measurable respects ours is the most successful civilization that ever existed. The average life span was never so long and what we have learned to call "the standard of living" was never so high nor enjoyed by so large a proportion of the population. By comparison with any other race that ever lived we are amazingly well fed, well clothed, and well housed. We suffer less physical pain, we enjoy more conveniences, and we know more about the laws of the physical universe in which we live. These are the things we have striven for and these are the things we have won. They may be more precarious than we like to admit, but we possess them. We are, or at least we seem to be, singularly blessed.

No previous civilization has ever before achieved so successfully its immediate aims because no other ever answered so successfully the questions it thought most important to ask

3

or solved so triumphantly the problems it thought most important to solve. To the achievement of the tangible goods we enjoy we have devoted almost the whole of our intelligence and our energy, and because the questions answered and the problems solved have centered around the achievement of power or the creation of wealth, man is now a creature more powerful and more wealthy than ever before. If a dissatisfied minority has persisted in expressing its dissatisfaction by calling us "materialists" we have usually replied, not so much by defending materialism as such, as in terms of a faith which is the very essence of modernity: namely, the assumption that material welfare is the *sine qua non* of every other kind and that every other kind may be expected to increase as the material does.

Old-fashioned philosophers often urged men to be wise, or virtuous or spiritual, first and either to despise material goods or to trust that they are to be won through wisdom and virtue; rather than, as we insist, the other way around. Man, we reply, may not live by bread alone but he certainly cannot live without it, and beyond that admission we hesitate to go—partly no doubt because we have reason in experience to fear that those who stress less tangible items in his diet are often preparing to deny him his bread.

Those who are disapprovingly aware that all this constitutes a novel emphasis sometimes call it "Americanism," though both as a theory and as a method it goes back to the seventeenth century, when "control of nature" was first proposed as the most important and most rewarding enterprise upon which the human race could embark. It is "American" only to the extent that here in the United States the method has been most successfully applied to even the smallest details of everyday life and most consistently put into the service of democratic and egalitarian ideals.

Ours is not only a powerful, a wealthy and a materialistic civilization, but also, within the limits imposed by its philosophy, an astonishingly kindly and generous one. This is an aspect of it which the conventional European critic is likely to leave out of account and, in all sincerity, fail to understand. Our "materialism" is a complicated and novel phenomenon the like of which he has never met before because, though his own civilization has been moving more slowly in the same direction, its philosophy has been less successfully implemented and its attitudes less tempered by kindliness or generosity. When such a critic says that we do not care about anything except money he is both right and wrong.

More than a century ago, De Tocqueville noted with amazement how American private citizens had a habit of spontaneously getting together to right some wrong or to relieve some need. He thought the phenomenon unique and he was probably right. Yet it has not only persisted but entered upon a new international phase. We are almost as distressed by suffering and want in distant places as we are by distress and want at home. And we are almost as determined to do something about it. No other nation in all history ever before gave away so much in money or goods. We seem determined to "do good" all over the globe.

Faced with these facts, the European critic shrugs. He hints that we have low, ulterior motives. Materialists, he thinks, would not be so generous. And since we are, by premise, materialists there must be a catch somewhere in all this generosity. Yet he often seems more puzzled than convinced by his own argument. Both European virtues and European vices are traditionally different from ours and he can't make us out.

What really troubles him (and might well trouble us) is something which he is not able to put into words and which the American has never felt any need to analyze because it is not, in his own experience, a paradox. That something is simply this: Materialism and stinginess, thinks the European, inevitably go together—and in his experience they usually have. But generosity and materialism are not at all incompatible—as the whole panorama of the American temperament abundantly demonstrates. We are not materialists in the sense that we love money for its own sake. We are not misers. We are spendthrifts who lavish wealth on ourselves, on our families, on our fellow citizens, and nowadays on the inhabitants of the four quarters of the globe. But we are materialists —generous materialists—in the very simple sense that we believe everything worth having can be had if we are willing to spend enough money to get it.

Nearly everything which makes American life both richer and poorer, both better and worse, than life in any other civilized community ever has been before goes back to the virtues and limitations of this generous materialism. We believe, for example, in education—more passionately and more uncritically than any nation ever believed in it before. We believe in it so thoroughly that we are willing to spend prodigious amounts of public funds. In nearly every American community, citizens vote to tax themselves at higher and higher rates to pay for the education of other people's children. But there are few to whom it ever occurs that putting more money into schools is not a sure way of getting more education, or that any deficiencies which happen to become manifest will not be remedied by putting more into school buildings. Being convinced that you cannot have what you refuse to pay for makes us generous; believing that you will get what you pay for, or at least that if you don't there is no other way of getting it, constitutes materialism.

Your true American never misses an opportunity to make money. He assumes that no one else does either. Perhaps, therefore, we actually are more devoted to the pursuit of the dollar than most other nations are to their pounds, francs, or marks. But we are not particularly anxious to hold on to it when we catch it. Acquisitiveness, not miserliness, is our vice. We are very ready to forgive a man for doing whatever is necessary to make a profit. We are quite resigned, to take small examples, to having the symphony concert interrupted by a commercial or the highway disfigured by billboards. We do not expect anyone to forgo a profit even if making it annoys everybody else. But we expect the profiteer to give generously to charity and to vote for public improvements which will cost him much more than he personally will ever get out of them.

The American is not being hypocritical when he tells you that he is frantically making money because he wants his children to "have all the advantages." He does. And he will spend freely the money he has made to buy these advantages; even, not seldom, to buy some of them for other people's children as well. He is not a materialist in the sense of being one who believes that education, travel, fun, even "culture" are foolish frills. But he is a materialist in the sense that he is quite sure no child can have "advantages" without having money to pay for them, and almost as sure that if he does have money to pay he will get the "advantages." Thoreau

7

thought money not required to buy one necessary of the soul. The typical American believes that no necessary of the soul is free, and that there are few, if any, which cannot be bought.

None of this is consciously cynical. If it were, our civilization would not be the world's wonder that it is: materially richer than any that ever existed before and providing a larger proportion of the population with a considerable share of that material richness than any other rich civilization ever did. In fact, our attitude is so far from being consciously cynical that not one American in ten can be made to recognize any inadequacy in "generous materialism" as a philosophy, a religion, or a way of life. He will call it merely "realistic" and "practical"; nothing more or less than "benevolence without humbug." He will sincerely suspect that anyone who so much as hints at a qualification is seeking an excuse for denying the common people their proper share of material things.

Only during the past hundred years have moral and social philosophers squarely faced the fact that it is easier—at least —to be law-abiding, well educated, and responsive to "the finer things of life" if you are not hungry and cold. Material welfare, they have decided, is a *sine qua non* for welfare of any other kind. But most Americans have taken a further step which does not logically follow, and despite the fact that Europeans still blame us, they and the rest of the world are following us as well as they can. We have forgotten that a *sine qua non* is not always the "one thing necessary" as well.

If the assumption has been turning out to be not so obviously true as was expected, not many will yet acknowledge the fact. Yet the vast majority of our well-fed, well-housed,

8

and well-clothed population has not turned toward intellectual or artistic pursuits, but has simply taken a greater and greater interest in even more food, even better houses, and even more expensive clothes. The more abundant its material riches have become the more thoroughly it has tended to believe that only material riches count. To those who have already a chicken in the pot and a car in the garage the next desirable thing to be acquired is less likely to be, say, a book than a television set and another car.

What philosophers used to call "the good life" is difficult to define and impossible to measure. In the United States today—increasingly also in all "progressive" countries—we substitute for it "the standard of living," which is easy to measure if defined only in terms of wealth, health, comfort, and convenience. But the standard of living does not truly represent the goodness of a life unless you assume that no other goods are real or at least that the less tangible and less measurable bear a direct functional relation to the tangible.

Even when measuring the standard as such we put greater and greater stress upon its most trivial and, indeed, most dubious aspects. A recent magazine article about Russia by one of the most widely read commentators on the world situation includes these remarkable sentences: "[In Moscow] the day-to-day routine of most citizens is inexpressibly dreary. No local citizen has ever read a gossip column or played canasta. No one has ever seen a supermarket, a drive-in movie, a motel or a golf course. Nobody has ever shopped by mail or paid a bill by check. No one has ever seen an electric toaster, a sidewalk café, a shoeshine parlor or a funeral home. I never saw a girl with dark glasses or encountered a Russian with a cigarette lighter."

Is life necessarily "inexpressibly dreary" without these things? Is our ability to supply them the best proof of the superiority of our civilization to that of Russia? If the answer to both the questions is "no," if these are not major, indispensable items in the good life, then it is obvious that either this writer (who has repeatedly demonstrated his ability to be understood and accepted by a large section of the more serious-minded public) has a wrong notion of what constitutes a high standard of living or the relation between such a high standard and the good life is by no means an identity.

Unless one is prepared to accept as inevitable such confusions as his, or to regard them as a small privilege to pay for prosperity and the other blessings of modern society, then it must appear that not even kindliness and generosity are sufficient to make the good life an inevitable consequence of wealth and power.

Wealth can come to be loved for itself alone, but also and more insidiously for the trivialities and vulgarities it enables one to obtain. Power can be used to oppress and abuse, but it can also become insidiously a threat to those who wield it and the occasion, as in the modern world it is, not of confidence but of an insecurity more acute than any powerful nation ever suffered from before.

Even those who recognize these paradoxes and are troubled by them are reluctant to consider the possibility that they suggest a revision of the fundamental premises which have made our civilization what it is. They may be both offended by the vulgarities of an almost too prosperous economy and frightened by threats which exist only because man has achieved so successfully the power he has for two centuries been seeking. They may even share Albert Einstein's doubt that the modern American is any happier than was the Indian whose continent he took. But they still take it for granted that if there is any right road it is the one we have been following.

If we are no happier than the Indians, that may be because some perversity in the human animal makes more than a certain degree of happiness impossible to him. If that is not the case, and if superabundant bread has so far created a society which only gossip columns and drive-in movies redeem from utter dreariness, then perhaps, so most people seem to believe, this is only because we need still more wealth still more equitably distributed. If power has not brought security, if indeed the most astonishing of new acquisitions has enormously increased the sense of insecurity, then perhaps what we need to know is how to "control nature" even more successfully. At least if none of these perhapses is true then few seem able to imagine any other which could be. Certainly few are prepared to abandon faith in wealth and power as such or able to imagine what else might reasonably be pursued instead.

Ours is not only the richest and most powerful civilization that ever existed, but also one of the most uneasy both without and within—within, perhaps because we feel some undefined lack in wealth and power; without, for a plain and simple reason.

Side by side with the optimism which success in achieving our immediate aims has seemed to justify, there has grown among intellectuals what some see as a perverse cult of despair and a readiness to accept as inevitable "the decline of the West." And though the average man certainly does not share this pessimism, he is likely to have heard enough about it and about the grounds upon which it is based to be puzzled by certain ambiguities.

On the one hand technology and that ability to "control nature" in which he so profoundly believes is so far from being in a state of decline that it still follows a sharply ascending curve. There are new worlds to conquer and space travel will begin tomorrow. Yet he cannot, on the other hand, fail to be aware that intercontinental missiles are already here and that our enemies may quite possibly have better ones than we have. Do these recent developments mark a new stage in man's triumphant conquest of nature or the beginning of the catastrophe with which a decline will end?

Progress is strangely mixed up with threats, and the release of atomic energy is, among many "firsts," the first technological triumph widely regarded as possibly, all things considered, a misfortune. To be sure, old fogies have always viewed with alarm. They thought twenty-five miles an hour in an automobile too fast; they shook their heads over the airplane; and it is possible that some conservatives among cave men were sure that no good would come of the wheel. But doubts about the atom are not confined to old fogies. They are shared by some of the very men who tinkered with it so successfully. The suspicion that man may at last have become too smart for his own good is nervously entertained in some very respectable quarters. Observing one of those bright new exploding stars called nova in the night sky, a famous American astronomer is said to have remarked with resignation, "Well, there goes another place where they found out how to do it."

The most prevalent opinion among our so confused contemporaries seems to be that tomorrow will be wonderful—that is, unless it is indescribably terrible, or unless indeed there just isn't any. *If* we are wise enough and lucky enough to escape all the various catastrophes which threaten, then there is no limit to the power and the glory ahead, no limit to the wealth, comfort, and convenience either. But the nagging "if" remains. Have we caught a Tartar or has the Tartar caught us? "He who rides a tiger does not dare to dismount."

There have been ages of hope and ages of despair before now. Historians of ideas inform us that for a thousand years nobody believed in Progress. They inform us also that the general opinion shortly before the year one thousand was that the world was about to end, although, five hundred years later, the notion that the possibilities open to man were limitless was already beginning to be widely assumed. But were the two opinions ever before held simultaneously and progress itself regarded as the possible cause of impending catastrophe?

A recent public relations advertisement by North American Aviation reads: "Supersonic supremacy is the absolute condition of America's future security. It is a day-to-day thing. It must grow with major advances." What we are being told—truthfully enough, it seems—is that we must run as fast as we possibly can if we are to remain where we are. The reward of heroic effort will not be some boon we never enjoyed before, and it will not be the conquest and enrichment which the proponents of military might used to promise. It will be merely the possibility of staying alive. This seems a rather insecure sort of security, though "security" is what it is here called.

If we turn to those of our contemporaries who are professionally occupied, not with the atom, but with the life of our fellow human beings, there is no escaping the fact that man as he appears in the most esteemed contemporary literature, American or European, is an unattractive creature and his life a distressing thing. Our novelists and poets may be wrong. Probably they do exaggerate somewhat and the majority of even their readers does not believe that either man or human existence is quite so unrelievedly dismal as they are made out. But at least this is what the most eloquent and respected among the writers do make out modern man and modern life to be.

It is true that the literary man as spokesman and prophet does not stand very high today even among the more educated classes. Any contemporary *Heroes and Hero Worship* would have to put the Hero as Man of Letters low in the hierarchy and the Hero as Man of Science at the top. But suppose we turn to these modern heroes. From some of the best of them you will get cold comfort. Here, for instance, is J. Robert Oppenheimer:

"Nuclear weapons and all the machinery of war surrounding us now haunt our imaginations with an apocalyptic vision that could well become a terrible reality: the disappearance of man as a species from the surface of the earth. It is quite possible. But what is more probable, more immediate and in my opinion equally terrifying is the prospect that man will survive while losing his precious heritage, his civilization and his very humanity."

Perhaps the physicists do have the best brains now functioning and it is something to have them used, as here they are, to think about man as well as about the things man makes.

Mr. Oppenheimer has reason to know that doing so has its dangers, and the eight leading scientists (including two Nobel Prize men) who consented some time ago to celebrate the centenary of Seagram's whiskey on TV by taking part in a symposium discussing the prospects for man a hundred years hence, were perhaps only playing safe when they confined themselves largely to predicting such blessings as delicious vegetable steaks, mail delivery from earth satellites, recreational resorts on space platforms, and machines which had abolished all physical labor. Thus they put themselves in the same class as those who write articles for the "service magazines" inviting us to drool over a future full of electronic cookers, family helicopters (at least two in every garage) and two-way household television-telephones *in color*. The most appropriate comment seems to have been that in the New York *Nation:* "The future of the human race resides in its humanity, not in its ability to construct honeymoon hotels on Venus."

But what is this "humanity" which the *Nation* is interested in and Oppenheimer fears we may lose? It is easier to say what it isn't or to define it negatively. It is that part of man's consciousness, intellect, and emotion which is neither exclusively interested in nor completely satisfied by either mere animal survival on the one hand, or wealth, power, and speed alone. It is that part of him which is least like a machine and therefore least satisfied by machines. It is the part that would like to know itself and that cherishes values to which nothing in the inanimate world seems to correspond and which the nonhuman world of living things only dubiously (though none the less comfortingly) seems to encourage.

Perhaps we are being a bit provincial to call this "humanness." Man existed for many millennia without, so we guess, exhibiting much of it. Perhaps Mr. Oppenheimer is right in supposing that he might endure indefinitely after he had lost it. Many contemporary men—and especially many contemporary youths—to whom only automobiles, airplanes, and television sets seem interesting, have already lost most of it. Perhaps it is primarily a phenomenon of recent man and, in the form we best understand, of Western man. Perhaps what some of us tend to call "the human being" first came into easily recognizable existence about the year 475 B.C. and began to disappear about seventy-five years ago. But though the world may soon belong to other creatures, there are some of us who cannot say simply, "Cultures come and go," without a regret for the passing of what seems to our possibly prejudiced minds more worthy of admiration than anything which ever existed before.

We need not, as some do, insist that the decision whether or not humanness in this limited sense will endure is wholly outside our power to influence. But there can be little doubt that the weight, the pressure, and the demands of the machine we have created make the preservation of "human" life more difficult than ever before—at least since the time when man ceased to be wholly at the mercy of the natural forces he has now mastered almost too well. If we should devote more of our time, energy, and brainpower to the cultivation of "the humanities" in the broad sense that our definition of "humanness" implies, then we would have to face the fact now so insistently urged upon us that "we need more scientists for survival," and that therefore much more rather than any less of the available brain power must be devoted to the machine and its management, to public education more and more exclusively devoted to "turning out the scientists necessary to our survival."

It may seem both frivolous and cynical to suggest that if neither we nor any other nation had so many or such successful scientists then we should not be so desperately in need of still more of them now! Yet in sober fact (and as is generally admitted), the greatest proportion of those we do need we need primarily to protect us against their fellow scientists in other lands. The monster we have called into existence must be looked after, and he is more demanding of time and attention than the creations of any other civilization. Even should we (as does not at the moment seem likely) become bored with it; even should we find ourselves feeling once again that art, philosophy, and what used to be called wisdom, are more interesting than either convenient or destructive machines—we might still not dare spend much time upon them. We are mounted on the tiger and it is hard to imagine how we might dismount.

There are many who give good reasons for believing that overpopulation is a threat to humane living second only to the domination of the machine. To them the technicians' assurance that with the desalting of sea water and the cultivation of algae in sewage pools (both of which are already practicable) we shall be able to feed a population many times the present, is not a promise but a threat. They say that what we need is not more men but better men and that there is no immediate prospect of getting them. But the question whether we should risk a stationary or slowly growing population, even if we should all become convinced that from a human standpoint it is desirable, still remains. Population pressures in other countries will make it all the more probable that they will use for aggression the long-range weapons man has supplied himself with, and hence it may well be that any nation not as numerous as it is physically possible for it to become is doomed to conquest by one or another of those bursting at the seams with expendable, more-or-less human beings. A cynical German might speak of the necessity of raising cannon fodder. We will call it only something like "providing for the optimum population from the standpoint of national security."

"Human condition" is a phrase enjoying at the moment a great vogue. In so far as it is more than merely fashionable or means more than simply "the present state of affairs," it must imply a distinction from something else—most legitimately, perhaps, a distinction between what *is* and what *might* or what *ought to be*.

Most current moral and sociological opinion sees little basis for such a distinction. To it the human condition is the only discussable, and, indeed, the only real, aspect of human nature or society. Society is presumed to be what it is as the result of an inevitable evolution, and human nature merely what a given state of society has made it. Any concept of human nature which implies something permanent, independent, and tending to revert to a norm is dismissed as a myth, since the so-called human nature could not be anything more than what the inevitable human condition at any moment has made it. "Good" and "bad" are assumed to be meaningless terms except in reference to some specific society or condition, and when you have described that condition you are thought to have said all that can be said upon that subject.

In the discussion to follow, the terms "human condition" and "human nature" will be so used as to imply a rejection of the assumption that the first is merely a product of the second. It will assume that, on the contrary, each is an independent reality and each is discussable as such.

Before explaining or justifying this assumption, we should first examine certain aspects of the human condition at the present moment.

·II·

The Condition Called Prosperity

t is generally taken for granted that you cannot have too much of a good thing, and in all the long history of our past, mankind has seldom had reason in experience to doubt this generalization. Most men at most times have had too little food, too little clothing, too few tools, and inadequate shelter. Nearly always they would have been better off, intellectually and spiritually, if they had had more. So undoubtedly would many individuals today.

Nevertheless, in the United States at least, a new paradox has intruded itself upon our already uneasy consciousness. Almost without realizing it we made, some years ago, the transition from that "economy of scarcity" which had been almost unbroken since the beginning of history to a new "economy of abundance." And no change in man's condition was ever more fundamental. Into our problem-ridden civilization came a new problem: superfluity. Is it possible that the pursuit of plenty, like the pursuit of power, can become too successful?

This novel aspect of man's condition seems to impose upon him certain necessities as ineluctable in their own way as those imposed by scarcity. Abundance has not so much freed him from the demands of circumstance as made him again its victim. Production is no longer a problem but consumption is, and the necessity of *consuming* enough becomes only somewhat less pressing than the difficulty of *producing* enough once was. We cannot use, we do not want, any more wheat and cotton and butter but we do not dare produce any less. And if the time should ever come when the super abundance of many other things was recognized as also a burden, physical or spiritual, we should find the dilemma indefinitely multiplied.

What we call prosperity depends upon continual expansion, especially of manufactured goods, and we believe that we cannot stop producing too much without finding ourselves soon incapable of producing enough. We do not see how we could limit the flow without so disrupting our economic system as inevitably to pass from superabundance to scarcity, and of two evils we not unnaturally choose the former.

That the Great Depression illustrated the workings of this paradox and was, indeed, the direct result of a failure to consume, seems pretty generally admitted. According at least to the Rooseveltian diagnosis, it was the consequence of "inadequate purchasing power" on the part of the majority and was to be cured by the relatively simple process of transferring the excess and unused purchasing power of the rich to the poor. The remedy seemed to work, and of all the methods ever suggested for meeting the problem it was the least paradoxical, as well as the most benign. "Overproduction," so it implied, was not absolute but relative, and was, in fact, the result, not of overproduction at all, but simply of inadequate distribution.

Once the pumps were primed the flow began. But inherent in the nature of the process is the fact that it cannot remain constant, that it must continuously increase or again start to dry up. And the question arises whether or not it is possible to arrange for sufficient consumption even by the whole population. Admittedly there are still individuals in want because distribution is not perfect. But it does not seem probable that even perfection would be enough, unless some method were found for increasing still further and indefinitely the number and quantity of things used up by the average man.

From this dilemma we were, so it is rather generally supposed, rescued first by the threat of war, and then by war itself. Though war is the greatest of all wasters, waste was, so it began to seem, not a threat to prosperity but an indispensable condition of it. "Waste not, want not" is a valid injunction only under an economy of scarcity. "Waste or you will want" is one of the most fundamental truths in the new *Rich Richard's Almanack*.

Few if any are hardy enough openly to advocate starting a war in order to preserve and increase prosperity, though anyone who desired to do so could certainly point to our economic history between the years 1939 and 1945. Up to the first of these dates the success of the Roosevelt experiment was hanging in the balance. But we emerged from the providential war more prosperous than ever before and with

23

prosperity more evenly distributed. Never had mass purchasing power been so great. Both absolutely and relatively the real wages of the worker, or average man, had never been so high. There was more wealth to share and he had a larger share of it than ever before.

It used to be said that wars were created by the rich in order that their profits might be increased. But this last war raised the workers' "standard of living" at least as spectacularly as it increased the profits of the capitalist, and unless the worker can be assumed to be less prone than the industrialist to think first of his material advantages, there seems reason to fear that we might someday be pushed into war by a mass demand for the higher real wages which it can bring.

No worker, capitalist, or theoretical economist has yet come quite to the point of recommending war as the most effective answer to the growing problem of overproduction, but the logic of such a solution is clearly enough implied by the fact that no current discussion of the economic outlook ever fails to raise the question of the possible effect of an easing of international tension or to ask what may be found to take the place of the salutary waste for which national defense is now responsible. Thus the most obvious answer to the problem of what seems to be too much of a good thing is, "Encourage every individual to consume as much as possible, and then waste as much as possible of what is left in defense or war."

There is, however, also a third remedy hardly less obvious that is tacitly given almost as often: "Increase the number of people consuming as well as the amount each consumes." Advertising executives exult in what one of them recently called "the bumper crop of babies," and they proclaim complacently their happy duty to see to it that as these babies grow up they are conditioned to all the "psychological needs" which advertising knows how to create.

Thus the sanction for the injunction "Increase and multiply" becomes, like everything else, ultimately economic. Of course the bumper crop of babies will grow up into producers as well as consumers, but we can still keep one generation ahead of disaster as long as the population continues not merely to grow, but to grow at an ever increasing rate. A few years ago *Forbes Magazine* printed the following paragraph:

"Lean crop of Depression babies is partially responsible for recent declines in whisky and cigarette sales as well, some industry men believe. 'Never before,' says one company president, 'have so few children reached the cigarette-smoking age as now.' But drink and cigarette makers are anxiously eying the years when the bumper crop of World War II babies—who are now helping dairy, food and shoe companies ring up record-breaking sales—become old enough to take up smoking and drinking."

A generation ago many psychologists, sociologists, and reformers were saying that since "planned parenthood" had at last become possible we were for the first time in a position to concern ourselves profitably with the question of how many children, born at what intervals, would create, under any given circumstances, the happiest, healthiest, and most promising families. But such questions have now become as irrelevant as they were before parenthood could be planned. We have solved the biological problem only to find ourselves faced by the economic. Unless families continue to get larger and larger, there seems to be little hope that a mere increase in per capita consumption can be sufficient for the needs of expanding industry—which must continue to expand or collapse. And thus in population as in so many other things it begins to appear that quantity, not quality, counts.

Such is at least one of the assumptions commonly made, and if, as the current cultural relativists insist, no society is good or bad in itself but only more or less successfully whatever it is, wisdom must consist in accepting ours for whatever it may become. If, in other words, the concept of the good life is meaningless unless defined merely as a successful adjustment to things as they are, and if human nature is so limitlessly conditionable that it may adjust itself to whatever condition it finds itself in, then a good life is as easy or as difficult to achieve in a society devoted exclusively to wealth and power as it would be in any other, and there is no reason why our children, if not we ourselves, should not contentedly accept a condition which requires men and women to breed primarily in order to supply the increasing number of consumers necessary for the proper functioning of the system of production which it is our first duty to maintain.

If, on the other hand, man has certain needs and desires which are not merely the creation of the condition in which he finds himself; if there is a good life and a good society to which he naturally aspires—then it may not be so easy as the cultural relativists suppose to adjust without resentment to a situation in which men are so much the slave of their Leviathan of production that its needs rather than their own determine their actions and their choices.

Suppose for example that they prefer peace to war or would rather wage war in the interest of what they regard as justice or a superior political system than merely in order to maintain production by increasing waste. Suppose also that they would rather base their estimate of an optimum population and the ideal size of a family upon convictions concerning the intellectual and emotional welfare of the children rather than accept the necessity of continually increasing the congestion in which we live because Leviathan demands it. In either case, at least one aspect of their seemingly so prosperous condition is one which promotes neither happiness nor certain other aspects of the good life.

Even those least capable of evaluating their condition in such general terms are sometimes dimly aware of it, or at least of the specific pressures brought upon them as individuals to live in the fashion which must be encouraged if the existing condition is to continue. Never before was the average man so continuously pursued by the paid (and now also the hidden) persuaders who urge certain actions upon him. That unfortunate advertising man who invented the vivid phrase "captive audience" soon regretted that he had revealed to the public his attitude toward it. But no disinterested sociologist had previously described so accurately or so vividly the situation in which nearly everyone finds himself. We are all permanently members of a captive audience from which we cannot by the most determined effort escape for long.

The rebellious may turn off the radio and refuse to install a television set. When they drive their automobiles they may keep their eyes steadily on the road in order not to see the parade of billboards urging them to buy, to do, or to consider carefully a thousand different things—including, comically enough, the debt of gratitude they owe to advertising. They may hesitate even to look up into the heavens above lest giant letters in the sky itself should urge them to buy one thing more. But they cannot hope to escape.

The newspapers or magazines they read in the privacy of their homes devote more space to "messages" from large corporations and specific suggestions from small ones than to news, comment, or fiction. And though the bus which takes them to work may not have in operation one of those commercial radio programs which were postponed by the unlucky frankness of the phrase "captive audience," the chances are that as the bus approaches they will see on its front "Pepsi-Cola" in letters much larger and more colorful than those which indicate where the bus is going.

Few of us like to be incessantly enjoined, urged, warned, or cajoled. We divorce husbands or wives who demand, urge, or beg in season and out. Yet we are not so closely captive to wives or husbands as we are to advertisers. And the time has long passed when we could complain of them as unequivocally an intolerable evil. Mere irritation is, to be sure, frequently expressed, and during the last few years serious protests have been made. In fact "Madison Avenue" has become one of the favorite whipping boys of the satirist and even of the reformer. But advertising is usually treated as though it were an isolated phenomenon and one which might be regulated or dispensed with without any modification of that concept of the good life which is responsible for the atmosphere in which advertising flourishes.

If we could convincingly accuse the advertisers of greed, or even of mere self-interest, we might reasonably ask why they should be allowed to invade our homes, destroy the beauty of the countryside, and deface the sky. But if "prosperity" as currently defined is the only reasonable meaning or measure of the good life, then a strong case can be made for the commonly accepted contention that when I am urged to trade in my car, buy a new washing machine, or try some new gadget, the profit motive of the seller is of less than secondary importance. Primarily, as he will eagerly explain, he is performing a public service by explaining to me my duty to support prosperity by behaving in the only manner by which this prosperity can be maintained. Or, to put it in another way, he is pointing out one major aspect of the present condition of mankind and urging me to "adjust" myself to it.

Once we accept the premise that "increased consumption" is the key to prosperity, and the premise that prosperity constitutes the highest ideal which either an individual or a society can pursue, then it is only reasonable that the advertisers' argument should be seconded by many economists and many statesmen. Thus one of the United States senators from a large western state was only voicing a commonplace when he recently urged a convention of advertising executives "to consistently improve its selling techniques" as a way of helping "to solve our problems," and he was only assuming as a self-evident fact that persuading people to buy and persuading them to want more and more material things constitute the first duty of our mentors. He was also only a little more frank than is usual when he went on to say: "Advertisers and advertising men must take a more active interest in schools . . . what is taught and how. Wherever possible they should participate in the classroom situation."

Educators have often been disturbed by the suspicion that what students hear in the classroom affects them very little by comparison with what they hear from the advertiser, who is in command of so many media. But it appears that at least one United States senator believes that what the advertiser has to say is so much more important than what education has traditionally taught that schools should surrender to him a good deal of the small influence they now exert.

One may be sure that not all teachers welcome such "participation in the classroom situation." But the National Educational Association, the largest and most influential organization of school men, seems eager to foster it. Two of its recent projects are a pamphlet called *Using Consumer Credit* and an elaborate "Outdoor Education Project." The pamphlet includes a cartoon (high-school pupils cannot be expected to read) captioned "Don't be afraid to use credit" and the Outdoor Education Project is built chiefly upon the use of guns and fishing rods. The first offers profuse thanks for the "generous assistance" of two collaborators whom it fails to identify as actually a couple of fellows who have been doing publicity for the National Consumer Finance Association, which turns out to be an organization devoted to promoting the interests of a group of small-loan companies. As for the Project, its "advisory committee" includes a president and a secretary-treasurer of the Sporting Arms and Ammunition Manufacturer's Institute, as well as the secretary-treasurer of the Associated Fishing Tackle Manufacturers.

If there is any distinction in a democracy between education and the propaganda of special interests, then one is bound to wonder how well the distinction will be maintained by the authors of the pamphlet on consumer credit or the advisory committee of the Outdoor Education Project. If the prevailing philosophy of education is sound, there is no reason why the distinction should be maintained. If it is not sound . . .

The year 1958 may go down in history as the year when Americans first began to manifest some dissatisfaction with two of the things they had been most proud of: their automobiles and their schools. Some of the chrome will probably come off both. But it would be a pity if reform stopped there.

Rephrasing in professorial gobbledegook what the statesman had expressed in the language of senatorial illiteracy, a Yale professor speaking shortly thereafter put it thus:

"As we shift from a society in which production is the focus of economic attention to one which is oriented to consumption, as we see a new pattern of personality emerging in American life, it seems to me that advertising as an institution moves into a position of influence comparable at least to a degree to such other major institutions for the formation of values as the school and the church."

Shorn of its verbiage, what this says is: As consumption becomes more important to our society, advertising will affect our lives as much as the school or the church. Put more bluntly it means: In a society where we make more than we can use, it is as important to persuade people to buy superfluities as to familiarize them with the best that has been thought and said.

Another professor is more bluff and hearty, at least in the newspaper report:

If Americans want a higher standard of living, all they have to do is to go out and buy it. It's there waiting for us.

That's the opinion of A. W. Zelmeok, a sort of triple-threat man in economics. He is an adviser for industrial buyers and for retail merchandisers and a visiting professor of marketing at the University of Virginia graduate business school.

"America stepped up its productive capacity tremendously during the war," he said, "then stepped it up again to help her allies. On top of that, $275 billion worth of plant and equipment has been installed in the last ten years.

"To keep all this functioning, to maintain constantly rising prosperity and to move the standard of living higher, consumers simply have to buy more."

Mr. Zelmeok is impatient with those who say we have a mature economy or who think great efforts are necessary to keep business on top of the present plateau.

"The public is far from being overstocked," he said. "Millions of families have only one car today; in modern living, one car to a family is no more practical than one pair of pajamas. The husband needs an auto to get to and from business, if not for use in business as well; the wife needs a car for suburban shopping, getting children to and from school, and carrying out other obligations. . . .

"Most of the nation's refrigerators should be replaced. Only a few kitchens have central, push button controls. A good part of our kitchens should be ripped out and replaced."

Moreover, such statements have been so generally accepted as useful and encouraging truths that an advertising executive could, without fear of raising any public indignation, proclaim recently to the public at large the following brilliantly frank statement of a current doctrine: "Perhaps the most dynamic and unique contribution of American economy to the world is . . . that, in a society which emphasizes psychological obsolescence, rather than physical wearing out of products [i.e. a society in which vacuum cleaners and automobiles are discarded not because they are not as good as ever but because their fins are in last year's style], we have helped to achieve the most productive economy in human history." Advertising, he went on to say, has been "a constructive and facilitative force in that economy. By creating a psychological desire to own—as opposed to that of necessity—advertising has increased the number of jobs available; raised the standard of living by reducing selling costs; increased company profits as well as security."

The question whether or not a society in which everybody's psychological needs for material things are being constantly increased and in which it is widely accepted as fact that economic health depends upon the number of things thrown away, is actually happier than one in which only real needs are met and goods are not replaced until replacement is actually rather than psychologically needed, is perhaps an unanswerable question. But it is a striking fact that in thousands of American homes the only magazines ever read or subscribed to are those devoted almost exclusively to suggestions for "improving" the kitchen, the living room, or the bathroom, so that the whole culture of such homes centers on them and the good housewife spends all the time left over from caring for her material surroundings in acquiring new "psychological needs"—i.e., in considering whether or not she ought to get different curtains, buy a new washing machine, or persuade her husband to invest in a different furnace.

A leading "woman's magazine" inserts in a leading "news weekly" the following advertisement of an article in its current issue: "Is Automation—the use of electronics to run machines—going to fill *your* home with pleasant surprises? Will 'magic eyes' light each room? Will you own a portable piano, cordless electric clocks—and a telephone you can answer without lifting the receiver? Discover how this exciting new development can make your home life happier." If this is not what the American dream has come down to, it is at least what many are trying to make it. The American woman is being told and is presumably ready to believe that what she needs to make her home life "happier" (astonishing word) is an electric clock without a cord and a telephone receiver which does not have to be lifted!

It is another striking fact that the "angle" adopted by the advertisements to which the text of most "home magazines" is merely a helpful supplement is not the *utility* of the thing offered but its value as a display. Leaf through any such magazine and you will be astonished to note how often even such once exclusively utilitarian objects as furnaces, washing machines, or even bathrooms are pictured, not in use, but as the owner is exhibiting them to neighbors. The appeal made is not, "Think how convenient or comfortable this or that gadget would make you," but, "Think how proud you will feel and how envious your friends will be when you show them what you have just acquired. You will not only have kept up with the Joneses but, for the time being at least, passed them by. And you will have served society by inciting them to emulation." After all, and as Bacon said, "The happiness of the great consists not in feeling that they are happy but in realizing how happy other people think they must be." In a civilization where it is not greatness but "a high standard of living" to which most aspire, Bacon's *aperçu* might well be adapted to read, "The happiness of the possessor," instead of, "The happiness of the great."

If wasteful consumption really has become the prime duty of the good citizen, and if persuading him to fulfill it is now the principal task of education and political leadership, then the senator and the paper previously quoted were as sound as the former was unoriginal in impressing upon the advertising men their moral obligation "to stimulate Americans' desire for better living" and in taking it for granted that "better living" means living in such a way as to require a more profuse expenditure of *things*. Better living in the sense of more peaceful, more contented, more intellectual, or emotionally more exalted living may be well enough in its way but it has no economic utility, and in so far as it would mean, for instance, more reading with less television viewing it would mean simply failing to assume one's proper share of the burden of consumption.

Perhaps, however, it is significant that the word "persuade" should be used, because it is only one of many more inescapable evidences of the fact that the teachers of this new morality are aware that present-day human nature does not spontaneously desire all the material things which our economic health demands that it should have. It may once have been necessary to restrain man's lust to own, to consume, and to waste; but this lust is no longer adequate to the needs of present-day industry. We cannot be trusted to buy enough things. In the public interest a vast co-ordinated effort must be made to sell them to us. Neither is it enough to satisfy mere "needs," even though it be recognized that such "needs" grow as they are fed. They still do not grow fast enough. They must be created; and it must also be recognized that many of them are not only created but are also in themselves "psychological." As the head of one large New

York advertising agency jubilantly pointed out, a study revealed that "of some 500 classified wants, only 96 were necessary." But what, in plain language, are "created psychological needs" except the desire for useless things which people have been persuaded that they want?

When Christianity proclaimed that not pride but humility was the source of all virtue, it asked the civilized world to accept what was perhaps the most drastic revision it was ever called upon to make in its ethical code. Second only to that is the transvaluation of moral values which the economy of abundance makes obligatory. Even Christianity continued to list prudence among the practical if not among the theological virtues; but a new generation which both inherits this long tradition and, during its own childhood, had drilled into it all the maxims inculcating thrift, economy, the avoidance of waste, and even, incredible as it may now sound, "doing without," is suddenly assailed from all sides by those who insistently urge it to spend what it hasn't got and who back up their injunction with threats of public calamity if the urgent advice is not taken.

Moreover, these urgings do not come only from merchants who have something to sell and who might therefore be suspected of having some merely private interest at heart. Only a few days before I wrote these lines, one of the most respected financial advisers devoted a column in a New York newspaper to the now familiar version of just this advice. The machinery of production, he said, shows preliminary signs of a slow-down. If you don't want prosperity to falter, then Buy, Buy, Buy—on credit, of course. In other words, the surest way of bringing on a rainy day is to prepare for it.

All prudential moralists used to agree that to live within

one's income was the first requisite for a materially secure existence, but prosperity now depends upon everyone's exceeding it. And all similar maxims have been similarly stood on their heads. Plain living, even if accompanied by high thinking, is a sort of treason—or un-American at the least. Conspicuous expenditure is no longer either vicious or even in bad taste; it is civic virtue. For your own as well as for the common good, go into debt as deeply as your creditor will let you. The new *Rich Richard's Almanack* bristles with aphorisms which can be formulated by the simple act of turning *Poor Richard's* upside down: "Waste or you will want." And as usual it was an advertising man who succeeded better than any economist or philosopher in reducing the new wisdom to an imperative that even the unthinking can grasp. For an air line peddling vacations on credit he invented a slogan which has everything—brevity, simplicity, and an irresistible appeal to the most childish of impulses. You may have read it a few years ago in almost any slick-paper magazine: "Have fun now; pay later."

No doubt there are those who will say that such phenomena are disturbing only to those who have failed to recognize the great modern truth, which is that virtues are always relative to a material situation and that, given the economy of abundance, materialism, conspicuous expenditure, waste, and improvidence have become, not private vices, but private as well as public virtues. But unless all moral truths really are relative to a material situation, if on the contrary there is anything permanent in either human nature or wisdom and virtue, then there is something which makes repugnant the injunction: "Love *things* above all else; learn to want more and more; waste rather than conserve; spend what you do not have." And it is repugnant in part, perhaps, because man realizes how prone one half of him is to do just that.

Take that simplest of formulations: "Have fun now; pay later." Let us grant for the sake of argument that the present situation really does make it wise and proper to put off until next year paying the bill for this year's vacation. How much further should the moral be generalized? How likely is one to conclude that in all situations and in respect to all kinds of fun it is wisdom to say, "Take the fun now and trust that tomorrow will pay?" Is there perhaps a general principle which rightly insists that such an attitude usually leads to calamity, and does the principle suggest that there is something undesirable in a situation where it seems inapplicable? If our present condition really does force upon us a pattern of economic behavior inconsistent with the pattern of behavior everywhere else advisable, then does that not suggest in turn that this condition, for all its smiling aspects, is somehow dangerous? Does it not suggest that even prosperity is not worth the price if the price involves violating those principles of wisdom which everywhere else are valid?

One thing seems clear. When man's first duty comes to be consumption, he suffers a strange loss of dignity, and not only he but the coming generation comes to be valued chiefly in terms of its potentiality as a voracious consumer.

At various times, various cultures have assigned their own characteristic reasons for believing in the sacredness of human life and in the value of each individual man. Once it was that every man had an immortal soul. In less religious but romantic ages it was usually that he had a unique personality. Then in societies dominated by utilitarian thought, it became that he could produce something. But now, at last, it is only that he can use something up. "Scorn not the common man," says the age of abundance. "He may have no soul; his personality may be exactly the same as his neighbor's; and he may not produce anything worth having. But thank God, he consumes. He eats baby food in infancy, begins to smoke and drink in adolescence, and understands psychological obsolescence when he grows up. He performs his essential function, and we honor him for it."

·III·

Permissive Exploitation

Of all the aspects of man's condition, the most obvious at any time is the abundance or scarcity of material goods. Some would, indeed, maintain that no other is measurable and that it is therefore the only one which it is scientifically legitimate to recognize. But there are many less tangible aspects, and some of them will be taken into consideration by all who believe that intangibles are worth discussing.

One may, for example, ask some such question as this: What proportion of any given society's time, effort, attention, and creative intelligence is expended upon the attempt to achieve positive goods; what proportion upon tasks recognized to be merely necessary efforts to stave off evils? Judging by such a criterion, it is evident that a society in which it is widely accepted as a fact that the major task it faces is the task of "defense," and that circumstances require us to subordinate everything else to that task, is not to that extent a very happy one. Given the circumstances it may be acting

41

wisely, but the human condition which it feels compelled to accept is obviously not desirable and the society not very good.

This is certainly the most striking example of the extent to which the prosperous American of today is not so fortunately placed as the prosperity itself might suggest. But it is not the only one and there are various other analogous situations in which he finds himself. He must, as has already been remarked, answer on the basis of something other than their intrinsic merits such questions as: Should population continue to grow at an increasing rate? and Should men be persuaded to love material things so much that they will go into debt to get them?

Many who refuse to consider passing judgment on the basis of a criterion involving so many intangibles are nevertheless ready enough to agree that the abundance of material goods is not the *only* measure of a good society and will willingly consider certain others. For instance: How equitably is the abundance distributed? And to what extent are some men exploited by others?

So far as the first question is concerned, one may say at least that no other wealthy society ever spread its wealth so widely. The second question cannot be answered quite so simply as many are inclined to assume.

Never before, it may be said, was the "common man" so free of obligation to serve the interests of the privileged. He gets a larger share than ever before of the wealth which his labors create, and the right to participate in the government of his nation by the casting of a ballot was never before so nearly universal and so real. At the same time this common man is also remarkably free in less tangible ways. Neither humble birth, rustic manners, nor other social inferiorities any longer prevent him from attending most educational institutions or from entering almost any profession. He is no longer scorned when he presumes to "ape the ways of his betters" but is praised instead for rising in the world and for demonstrating the excellence of the American Way. Far less than in many other nations nominally democratic is there any elite which attempts to impose upon him its tastes in art, literature, or entertainment. Libraries as well as publishers, even many schools and colleges, are eager to give him, not what some elite thinks he ought to have, but what he says he wants. The public-opinion poll designed to furnish reliable evidence of his desires, tastes, preferences, and even prejudices is one of the most characteristic features of our society and it testifies to the seriousness with which we take the will of the people—intellectually and artistically as well as politically.

Despite the extent to which all this is true, the desire to exploit is deep in human nature and, like many another of the less amiable aspects of that nature, is not easily frustrated by political or social institutions. Men may be declared legally free and equal but ways within the law are found to mitigate that freedom and that equality. Neither wealth nor birth is supposed to confer special privileges, but both do. Knowing the "right people" is a help even in democracies, and so it goes. Only the very naïve would suppose that exploitation could be completely abolished. But the question remains how important an aspect of the present condition of man it is; whether man is, today, as free from it even relatively as is often assumed.

43

Obviously the grosser and least disguised forms of exploitation do not flourish and are not taken for granted as they usually have been. The slave is gone, the indentured worker and the peon have disappeared from most areas in the United States, and labor unions have found ways of making the theoretical right of the worker to leave a job for which he is inadequately paid a real and effective right—as it often was not in the past. In fact, a major part of all the social legislation enacted since the beginning of the century has been sincerely designed to prevent either direct or indirect exploitation.

There is, however, another approach to the whole question of the role which exploitation plays in determining the present condition of man. We may ask, not what the laws are and the extent to which they achieve their purpose in preventing the more familiar kinds of exploitation, but instead a more sweeping question. We may ask to what extent the average man has been *persuaded* to lead a certain kind of life by people who profit directly from that kind of life and are, in various ways, responsible for the fact that he leads it; for the fact, indeed, that he *chooses* to do so.

If we try to answer this question, it may come to seem that even "psychological obsolescence" and the use which may be made of the concept represents a contribution to social dynamics hardly less important than another discovery which may be the most revolutionary of our time: the discovery, that is to say, that exploitation *by persuasion* may be made more profitable than exploitation by *force majeure*.

If, for example, you can persuade ten million people to buy some useless article or to pay ten percent more for some useful one than for another differently packaged or less ingeniously publicized, you can profit a great deal more than you could by paying labor substandard wages or even by buying slaves to cultivate your cotton patch. The victim pays willingly what it would be much more difficult to extract as rent, tax, or any other *droit du seigneur*. The sum is small, but ten million small sums add up to a great one for the exploiter, while for him who pays, a hundred such small exactions also add up to a considerable one. Upon such picayune chicaneries many modern fortunes are built. A whole science of exploitation by persuasion has grown up and the practice of it has become the profession of thousands. Indeed, the existence of this science and of this profession is by now a major factor in determining what the present condition of man is, and its importance grows daily.

No doubt its beginnings are almost as old as organized commerce. Even in ages when the overseer's lash was still exploiting slaves, the seller of medical nostrums plied his minor trade. But the selling of snake oil or wooden nutmegs was merely a piece of comic rascality, not a major factor in the economy of the country. It could not become a major factor until the creation of false values had become the realizable aim of a psychological science and until the development of the mass media of communication provided a vast audience upon whom the refined wiles of the modern barker could be practiced.

The old-fashioned medicine show with two kerosene lamps flaming at a cart-tail while a blackface banjoist softened up a rustic crowd before which some seller of nostrums would later make his pitch, was not a very effective device. In that day, really profitable exploitation had to take more obvious forms. The one-sided law, the threat of starvation, and the institution of open slavery provided more attractive opportunities to anyone not content with the smallest of profits.

Who would ever have dreamed that from the medicine show would spring the million-dollar TV spectacle, with the most popular and highly paid comedians and singers performing before an audience composed of a considerable proportion of the entire population of our country and at the behest of some merchant? Who would have guessed that, thanks to all the ingenious tie-ins between advertising, entertainment, the popular arts, and the great corporations the time would come when one of the most obvious aspects of the condition of the average American man is simply this: Most of the news he hears, most of the music he listens to, and most of the drama he witnesses—in fact almost all the intellectual or artistic experience he ever has—is provided by medicine shows. Even when he reads popular magazines he is still getting what the advertiser wants him to be given, and he buys not only his breakfast food but his automobile and probably, if he can afford one, his wife's fur coat also at one or another of his favorite medicine shows.

This is certainly pleasanter than being "scourged to his dungeon." The exploiters are certainly right when they say that the victim thinks he likes it; and if there really is no good nor ill but thinking makes it so, then perhaps the condition in which the victim finds himself is as good as any other. But at least such is actually his condition, and the great economic discovery of our times is that no form of exploitation has ever been so profitable as this new form which consists in convincing the mass of men that they want to lead the kind of life most profitable to a given industry or profession.

Permissive Exploitation

The defenders—say rather the celebrants—of advertising as one of the institutions most clearly responsible for the good life we are said to enjoy, always argue that the immense sums spent upon it are so far from costing the citizen anything that they actually reduce the price of the articles advertised by creating a mass demand which makes the economies of mass production possible.

So far as many trivial articles—lipsticks, perfumes, toothpastes, many "brand-named" foods, etc., go, this is simply not true—and the sum of the trivialities is considerable. So far as such major articles as automobiles, electric refrigerators, washing machines, and the like are concerned it probably is. But the really significant point is not the cost of these articles. It is rather that when the average man (and the average woman) is persuaded that his status in the community depends upon his recognizing "psychological obsolescence" and buying what he does not need, he is being exploited in the interests of both the seller and that conception of prosperity which only extravagant expenditure can preserve. It is not that he pays too much for the "fins" and styling of this year's automobile, but that he is persuaded to pay anything at all for them.

It may even be true, as one defender of advertising has recently maintained, that the woman who pays double for a widely publicized lipstick, admittedly no better than a cheaper one, actually gets her money's worth in the psychological satisfaction inherent in feeling that she belongs to the class which "can afford the best." But are such satisfactions as these very desirable ones, and is the condition of man improved when they come to play a larger and larger role in the good life at which he aims? We should, so Bernard Shaw

47

has warned, be very determined to get what we want because otherwise we will find ourselves wanting what we get. To take advantage of that law is the great strategy of the advertiser.

When the old masters of the common man did not use force, they bade him submit to the divine right of the dominant to dominate; but the new grand principle is "Give him what he wants—at a sound profit." Thus the method is, to borrow a term from the child psychologists, the "permissive method." The early philosophers of liberalism thought the common man should be elevated. Only the Tories used to feel that they could get more out of him by keeping him ignorant. But that is precisely what his new masters have again come around to. To themselves (and in moments of frankness even to the public) they say, "I can get more out of you by pandering than by bossing." They brutalize him by appealing to his lowest tastes and his vulgarest appetites. "Just tell me," they implore, "what you want and I will give it to you—at a profit."

Moreover, and despite all their occasional pretense at elevating taste by small doses of "high" art and literature, they know very well what they are doing. Here, for instance, is the attitude of Mr. Max Wylie as expressed in his book *Clear Channels,* published while he was associated with (of all things) the "TV-Radio Workshop," which was, in turn, sponsored by the Ford Foundation: "Television isn't going to bring culture to a lot of people who don't want any more than they now have, and who haven't room to store it if given it. And television shouldn't try to do this, and it isn't going to try to do it."

Old-fashioned democracy went on the assumption

(whether right or wrong) that the common man did have "room to store" more "culture" than he was getting, and it was determined to test the hypothesis by making more and more available. The new "permissive" democracy goes on Mr. Wylie's assumption that the common man has no such available room and that the kindest thing to do is not to embarrass him with a realization of the fact. The procedure is said to make life more agreeable for the common man and it is certainly more profitable for those who would practice this painless exploitation.

For the old-fashioned kind of exploitation which democracy has striven so persistently to eliminate, the exploiter's first requirement was an adequate brutality. For the new, the exploiter needs first a boundless cynicism, and second a humility (shall we call it?) which makes him willing to descend to small tricks of which any robust robber baron would have been ashamed. Recently, for instance, he has discovered a new opportunity. Even if the average mental age is, as he has boasted, fourteen, fourteen is still fourteen and represents a maturity too advanced to be taken in by many of the tricks which occur to the exploiter's ingenious mind. Obviously the next step is to see what can be done with those real children who have not reached even this level of understanding. And, as is well known, some of the most elaborate current campaigns are directed against these innocents. Confections and various other articles of food are packaged in such a way that a small child can easily recognize them, and then, over the child's TV program, he is urged to help mama do her shopping at the super market by collecting the package with so-and-so's picture on the front. Poor mama was already fighting a losing battle to buy what she judged to be better, cheaper, or more wholesome rather than what some synthetic cowboy or persuasive puppet had been urging junior to urge her to buy. Now she is faced with a *fait accompli*. The article she doesn't want is already in the wire cart which is the modern version of the market basket. And we boast that our laws no longer permit the exploitation of children!

Or take another example. Recently an unctuous voice has been wheedling infants by asking the question, "Where do we keep our candy?" and then answering it with, "In our rooms!"—i.e., where we can eat it when and as often as we want without any tiresome protest from mama about spoiling our appetites or rotting our teeth. Taking candy from a baby used to be the phrase to describe one kind of exploitation on its lowest level; giving candy to a baby—more of it than is good for him—typifies the new. It's what he wants, isn't it? Democracy demands that we give the people, even the youngest people, what they want, doesn't it? Besides, you can give your child vitamin pills (the next sponsor will tell you about them) and you can demand that the city fluoridate his drinking water (which you will hear all about in the panel discussion presented next hour "as a public service").

The pettiest of these tricks are played to sell the inexpensive items of daily consumption, but the method is the same in promoting even the most expensive luxury items, as well as all the machines and conveniences of modern living. Nor are the appeals very different. Buy A rather than B; it costs more but by buying it you can demonstrate to your neighbors that you can afford to pay more. You can join the company of men of distinction simply by drinking a certain whiskey or even by using a certain shaving lotion. Still another catch-penny luxury is also for those who want the best and can pay for it. Buy it or you are confessing either that you think the best is too good for you or that you can't afford it. And if you confess to either, your neighbors will quite properly look down on you.

Mrs. Grundy used to be concerned largely with morals. Her whispering campaigns used to hint that a man beat his wife or was unduly attentive to some other man's wife. Now she whispers: "The Smiths are still poking around in their old last year's car. Mr. Jones doesn't have that expensive smell about his jowls after shaving. Mrs. Williams' sheets are dingy."

What all this does to the exploiters is almost as horrible as what it does to the exploited, because it reduces them to a condition highly repugnant to human nature, one result of which is the bitterness and savagery exhibited by those who finally do speak out and describe in article or novel the inner and outward lives they lead. To be compelled to wheedle those whom you despise is one of the most corroding of all humiliations. No man who chooses to do it can help despising himself. And yet that is precisely what the advertising man, the TV tycoon, and the Hollywood big shot have chosen to do.

No other explanation is necessary for the pictures they sometimes draw of their own world. They have wealth and power. They are successfully exploiting what Hollywood used to call "the peasants." But they are also licking boots and cringing before the slightest frown of "the peasants." The ruthless, public-be-damned tycoon at least kept his scornful pride. But his day has passed and the day of the sycophant has succeeded. Now the really successful man is more like the classical parasite than like a robber baron. And he despises himself because he can be neither sincere nor reckless. His is the self-hatred of the professional flatterer whom the real masters load with favors for a time but may at any moment kick out. He tells himself that he is powerful but he knows that he really is not. He serves a master whom he despises. He is the overrewarded court jester and court pander at the democratic court.

No other relationship so surely curses him who gives and him who receives. No other form of exploitation more completely destroys the exploiter as well as the exploited. Is it any wonder that so many of the intellectuals who play the role first blame the "social system" and then, sometimes, join some radical group in an effort to justify themselves *to* themselves? How convenient it is to be able to blame a lack of integrity on a "historical situation" instead of on oneself.

In an ecstasy of impudence the spokesmen for the new techniques of exploitation sometimes describe their methods as essentially those of education—not in the narrow scholastic sense but in that sense now so popular among the teachers of teachers. Schooling, so they say, is now generally admitted to be no mere matter of the three R's in the elementary grades and of book learning in the higher. It is, indeed, not primarily a matter of the intellect at all. It is not learning facts or even how to think. The teacher's chief aim should be instruction in the art of living in a particular society—should be, if your vocabulary extends that far, a process of "acculturation." This being the case, the advertiser can play an even more important role in the educational process than the schoolteacher. He has more money at his disposal; he reaches a larger audience; and he can hire the most skillful practitioners of the art of persuasion.

The world in which the child will live is, so he says, a world in which nothing is more important than the various goods which the advertiser has to sell. Since preparation for life means nothing more clearly than an acquired familiarity with his environment, it is evident that what the pupil needs most to know is what is available and where he can get it —as well, of course, as how to swim in the current of the new economics.

Who can teach him all these things better than the advertising man, who is in close touch with the makers of these various articles which will define his environment? Who, for that matter, can teach him better the few abstract principles he will need to know? The school will, for instance, teach certain aspects of loyalty, like loyalty to God and country, though the "institutional" advertisement is actually taking over that also. But until the advertiser is given a more direct part to play in the school system itself, another kind of loyalty, no less important, must be taught by the advertiser himself—namely brand loyalty, or the refusal to be seduced from your devotion to a particular mark of goods. As an agency has just reminded its clients, brand loyalty is "a substantial asset . . . In other words, Mr. Bizman, protect that loyalty by constantly courting your consumers." Let children every morning say to themselves (or better yet, say publicly), "I pledge my allegiance to my flag, to my country and to Ootsitoots the whole-grain, toasted, sugared, body-and-soul-building cereal."

At the moment when these pages were being written there began to appear in current newspapers and magazines the first ominous references to growing evidence that the prosperity we had been enjoying since the end of the war was again beginning to falter. Population was continuing to grow at an unprecedented rate; wages were continuing to rise and thus to increase mass purchasing power; government expenditure on "defense" had shot up to unexpected levels. And yet, for all that, not enough manufactured goods were being consumed or wasted to keep the factories operating at full capacity or all the factory workers employed.

The major political parties were vying with one another in declaring their ability and their determination to nip this "recession" in the bud and to prevent it from becoming a "depression." But neither any influential political spokesman of either party nor any organ of opinion with mass influence suggested any action not based upon the assumption that more spending and more consumption by someone or other is the obvious and only remedy. The simple assertion that all would soon be well again if everyone could be persuaded to plunge deeper into debt in order to buy things he does not need or very much want was repeatedly made, and though not all the proposals were so naïve, they all had a great deal in common. *Life* Magazine reassured its readers with a long and elaborate discussion of what it called "our built-in remedy for depression" and folksily identified it as babies. Elaborate statistics were provided to show how "bumper" the present crop is and how delightfully expensive babies are when you count not only their clothes and their food but their doctor's bills and their toys. It seemed no

here to consider the possibility that prosperity might be
important because of babies, rather than that babies exist
primarily to maintain prosperity.

To the best of my knowledge, no widely heard voice ques-
tioned any of the fundamental assumptions. All took it for
granted that the economy of abundance had created one
problem and one problem only, and that an ever increasing
consumption of material goods is the only possible solution
of it. Prosperity, like the other creations of technology, is a
tiger whose riders do not dare dismount.

In a televised speech the President went no further than
to advise his audience to "Buy what you need"—without
suggesting even vaguely how "need" might be defined. Other
members of our government were less cautious, and advertising agencies confessed frankly to their customers that
"buying what you need" is not enough. Here, for instance,
are excerpts from a little sermon published in an agency
house organ:

Psychologically people are "Puritans" at heart . . . even in our
free-spending society . . . the belief that a frugal life is best
still remains in the subconsciousness of many. . . . Management,
sales personnel and advertising must . . . aim their persuasive
talents toward re-educating people's thinking into healthier channels. Show them it is their right to enjoy life. Try to show [the
housewife] she does not have to live up to yesterday's exacting
standards of what a housewife should be . . . People are buying
but they could buy more. They're just afraid to . . . Let's enjoy life . . . Out with the "puritanical" thinking that doing without is being "good" . . . that postponing a purchase until later
is the "right" thing to do. . . . If buying a better life be a "moral"
sin . . . let's sin a little . . . and live a lot!

By common consent, the most important thing we wer
not buying enough of was automobiles. Said the headlin
and subheads on a *New York Times* article (May 25, 1958)
"When Autos Lag, All U. S. Feels It. Industry Involves Mi.
lions of Americans. New Cars Take 10% of Income. A Bi
Source of Taxes. Absence of a Spring Upturn Concerns Fa
removed Areas of Economy."

Of the fact there is no doubt. But how sound or how s
cure is a prosperity which threatens to collapse just be
cause many people seem a little less ready than last year t
discard automobiles on which not even the chrome has be
gun to tarnish and to buy new ones on credit? The questio
is no longer what people need but what "the econom
needs; and if most citizens are not willing to go further int
debt to buy what they do not need they must be persuade
to."

What are automobiles for? Not, as you might think, pr
marily to take you somewhere or even just to ride aroun
in. They are primarily to "support the economy" by employ
ing labor and using up materials. If you bear that fact clearl
in mind, you will not ask why they should be so big, s
powerful, or even why they have to have grotesque and awk
ward fins. People do not need them; but industry does. Eve
the fins consume metal and employ labor. Things are in th
saddle and ride mankind to a degree and in a fashion Emer
son never dreamed of. "This," said a big leader of the in
dustry, "seems to be hate-automobiles year." But few Amer
cans hate automobiles. At most what they exhibited was
mild, not clearly understood, revolt against the demand tha
they should be ridden by automobiles instead of riding i
them.

Permissive Exploitation

One of the oldest, most inclusive, and most familiar of socialist criticisms of the "capitalist system" is that it encourages production, not for use, but for the profit of "the bosses." There is much in the charge even under welfare capitalism, but in a different way. Production is now neither for use nor exclusively for the profit of the bosses. It is for the "prosperity" of labor and the average citizen. But the "needs of the economy" rather than his own genuine needs still come first. And neither socialism nor communism seems to know how to reverse that topsy-turvy order.

Referring to a depression in his own day, Thoreau once wrote to a friend: "If thousands are thrown out of employment, it suggests that they were not well employed." To most readers who come upon that casual remark for the first time it seems merely heartless: "If there is no useful work for these thousands of people to do, then just let them starve." But there is another way of looking at it. If you are thinking not only of their plight but of how they came to be plunged into it, then Thoreau's remark goes straight to the heart of the matter. A major fraction of the population is engaged in making things which nobody needs. All the arts of publicity are proving insufficient to persuade a sufficient number that they even "want" them. Is there nothing better that the now unemployed could have been working at? Must they boondoggle on a gigantic scale? Must boondoggling be accepted as the foundation of our economy? Or are there tasks upon which all might be "well employed"? Is our definition of what constitutes the good life the real reason they are not?

If a large part of what is good as well as bad in man's present condition derives from his technological development, it is also true that to most people that development seems to be and to have been inevitable. Science and industry seem to lead independent lives of their own and to obey certain laws of growth. Both the nineteenth-century industrial revolution and the atomic revolution of the twentieth century seem to have "just happened." When the time was ripe, when science and invention had taken the necessary preliminary steps, the next step followed inevitably. Could the Little Englanders, no matter how numerous they might have been, have prevented the growth of the British Empire once steam was turning the looms, once the looms were crying out for cotton, and for an increased population to which the woven cotton could be sold? Suppose Rousseau had been ten times more convincing than he was. Would not civilization have gone on getting more complex instead of simpler? Do not our knowledge and our inventions sweep us along in their current?

We may, so we tend to think, solve some of our problems, but we are powerless to change the form they have taken. To some extent we may plan what uses we will make of power and how goods will be distributed. But we do not believe that the statement of the problem was ever within our power. We may choose socialism, communism, New Deal capitalism, or unlimited competition. For the wisdom or folly of that choice we are responsible. But it is commonly assumed that no human choice was responsible for the condition with which we have to deal.

If all this is correct, then such wide-ranging discussions as the present are merely frivolous. It might still be worthwhile to make specific suggestions, to debate socialism versus capitalism or, to be even more specific, commercial radio versus government sponsorship. But it would not be worthwhile to raise the general question whether or not ever increasing productivity and an economy which is becoming an economy of superfluity creates an undesirable condition for man. That condition would then be taken as a thing given, not a thing chosen, and unless a critic is ready to propose a solution, unless he can tell us what political or social moves should be made if we want to be saved, he might better spare his breath.

Only if it is assumed that the problems now presented were *not* inevitable but are the result of choices made one after another, and that the problems of the future will be those which we are at the moment preparing by the choices we make now, is it important to understand what choices have been and are in the making.

As Henry Adams so insistently pointed out, neither cathedrals nor railroads "just happened." They were the major enterprises of two different ages because each age was convinced of the fundamental importance of what it was doing. There was an identifiable epoch of comparatively recent history when the faith which led to railroads (as well as to so much else) was born. It was the age when, for the very first time, men realized that they could alter rapidly and radically the material circumstances of human life. Until that time it had been taken for granted that these circumstances could be changed only slightly. There could be good government or bad; one system of agriculture was somewhat more productive than another; poverty might be more or less deep and the necessity for labor almost up to the limit of human endurance might be mitigated. But the possibility of transforming the physical conditions of human life by mastering the laws of nature was a new possibility. When men did realize this possibility, Western civilization committed itself to the task so whole-heartedly that it brushed almost everything else aside and gradually developed the general conviction that whatever else was good must come automatically as the control over nature increased.

When Bernard Shaw said, "The only trouble with the poor is poverty," he was only reducing to its simplest and most unqualified terms what had long been a dominant faith in the more general form of, "Man needs nothing except an increase in his ability to wield power and produce goods." So firm was that faith that we have ceased except incidentally, and, as it were, with the little ability and determination left over, to concern ourselves with the other ways in which the human condition might be either improved or prevented from deteriorating. And no radical improvement in the condition of man is possible without some modification of this exclusive emphasis.

Scientists have recently begun to talk a good deal about the neglect of fundamental research. Too much, so they say, we are devoting ourselves to the solution of present problems, and to the utilization of accumulated knowledge. We give too little time and energy to the pursuit of truths whose usefulness or applicability we cannot see.

Their arguments are convincing, but do they not apply also beyond the field of science? If we do too little fundamental research, do we not also do too little fundamental thinking? It is all very well to ask what laws ought to be passed, what courses ought to be taught in schools, in order to correct some of the evils which have developed in man's present condition. But we need to consider more thoroughly what that condition is. We need to ask questions about it, such questions as this discourse is attempting and will continue to attempt to ask. The justification for them is, not that they always suggest immediate solutions, but that they probe into a situation which will need to be understood before practical solutions can begin to be thought about.

Are we so much at the mercy of our system of production only because we have been too exclusively concerned with production? Is the trouble with the poor and the rich alike something besides either poverty or superabundance? Are certain of the present concrete problems unsolvable because the tendencies which produced them are producing others more rapidly than they can be solved? Is mankind too "realistic" for its own good?

Such questions are at least worth raising. If they can all be answered in the negative, it would at least be well to know that they can—that they have been thought through —before we continue at an accelerated pace along the path we have been following. Is some modification of our aims desirable; is our commitment to the enterprise to which the seventeenth century first committed itself too absolute, or has it continued too long? Is a civilization without cathedrals as unbalanced as one without much else?

It is easy enough to point to those civilizations which did refuse to accept the challenge of technology. It is easy enough to ask, "Do you want to be China or India?" These countries demonstrate what disdain for the material and the practical leads to. The "wisdom of the East" is to live in want, squalor, and disease. But is it really necessary to choose one extreme or the other? Is it impossible to believe in wisdom without neglecting power? Is it impossible to produce a tolerable "standard of living" unless you permit it to demand, "Thou shalt have no other gods but Me"? Perhaps if the answer is "yes," then we will or even should choose to have none other. But until we have got an answer which cannot be doubted, it is still worthwhile to ask the question.

·IV·

The Human Surplus

While those whose chief concern is to "maintain prosperity" rejoice in the prospect of limitless human fertility, there are others who fear that the bumper crop of babies is already a surplus, and in a recent popular article Arnold Toynbee put the stamp of his prestige upon two familiar propositions. Like nearly everybody else he believes that another world war would destroy civilization. And like a great many, at least, he believes also that if a major war is avoided overpopulation will soon threaten the very civilization that has been saved. Too few people are going to be left if we have a major war; too many will soon crowd the earth if we do not. And that seems to constitute as neat a pair of horns as any upon which the poor puzzled man of good will was ever tossed.

A cynic might suggest that the conclusion is obvious: what we need are wars of precisely the right size. Perhaps if "progress" had stopped with TNT and Napalm they would have conveniently taken the place of those famines, pestilences, and diseases of infancy which once supplied the natural checks. Unfortunately, perhaps, "progress" did not stop there, and any world government powerful enough and wise enough to prevent war on a global scale will have to make other arrangements for the prevention of overpopulation.

When the population got too dense for comfort in any given region it might, for instance, license sportsmen from neighboring countries to thin it out. This would furnish healthy recreation for the hunters and if a bag limit based on an accurate estimation of population density was set, that density would soon be reduced to an optimum. Thus the necessary elimination of the socially undesirable could become a source of innocent merriment for the others. The method is now commonly employed by the game managers of some public lands and some of them say it works very well.

Any squeamishness which might be felt at first would no doubt be soon conquered. One of Shaw's characters remarks that all biological necessities soon become respectable and a great many sober social scientists seem to agree that "moral" and "immoral" have no meaning except in the context of the social needs of a community. How then could they object *a priori* to a plan which would provide a sportsman's equivalent of war?

Unfortunately, those of us who have never been able to mature a genuinely realistic view of things and who still have a lingering, irrational reluctance to break the taboos of our tribe find this logical solution of the problem somewhat less than satisfactory even though we are not prepared to come up with a glib one that is.

Once, of course, we just said "birth control" and let it go at that. We were sure that if the birth of a child were not something which happened but something which was willed, then there would never be any more children than could be properly fed and housed. Obviously, however, it does not work out that way, and it is plain enough by now that, for whatever mysterious reasons, the birth rate does not necessarily fall when methods of controlling it are available.

In the United States the birth rate is said to be approximately the same as that in India, where the "planned parenthood" movement is just getting under way. In Ireland, on the other hand, where the laws against the dissemination of information concerning contraception are fanatically stringent, the birth rate has fallen so low that the very existence of the Irish race in Ireland seems threatened. How accurate these figures are I do not know; but the trends are unmistakable and it is obvious that both those who hoped for salvation and those who feared race suicide, wildly overestimated the effect which birth control would have.

Does it seem quite safe to say that we in America will face the problem when we come to it and that we quite properly refuse to worry about the possibility of too many people when it looks rather more likely that there won't be any at all? Too many (and there are already too many in a great many places) is certainly one cause of those very wars which threaten to leave too few. We could, of course, put the whole question up to Time and Nature, but it is one of the distinguishing peculiarities of the human mind that it is often not well pleased with the summary solutions which Time and Nature do supply in their own rough-and-ready fashion to this and other problems.

No one can say that the problem itself has gone unrecognized. It has recently been discussed in a number of very able books like Sears' *Deserts on the March*, Cook's *Human Fertility*, Sir Charles Galton Darwin's *The Next Million Years*, and Harrison Brown's *The Challenge of Man's Future*. Facts and statistics are readily available. Moreover, and with almost monotonous regularity, general surveys of our probable future say substantially what Toynbee said in his popular article. Yet only a minority of those accustomed to consider the state of the world seem actually to take the situation very seriously and it is frequently disregarded even when it is obviously relevant.

According to the calculations sponsored by the United Nations, world population increased from 1,810 million in 1920 to 2,734 million in 1956; is now increasing at the rate of forty-four million per year; and promises to continue to accelerate. In the undeveloped countries the falling death rate accompanied by an increasing birth rate is especially striking. In Ceylon, for instance, though it is already a densely populated country, the aid given by the World Health Organization is partly responsible for a decline in the death rate from 20.3 to 11 per thousand within ten years. Here the birth rate remained nearly stationary, but in Puerto Rico the death rate in 1955 was 7.2 while the birth rate had risen to 35.

What the effect of aid from the outside can be when it helps more people to stay alive without lowering the rate at which babies are born is illustrated by Sir Charles Galton Darwin in his *The Next Million Years:*

"Not long ago the [Indian] province of Sind was mainly desert; the ground was quite fertile but there was no rainfall. A great engineering undertaking, the Sukkur barrage has spread the waters of the Indus over a very wide area and turned much of the desert into a garden. According to

66

universally accepted standards this was a great benefit to the world for it made possible the adequate feeding of a people previously on the verge of starvation. But things did not work out like that, for after a few years the effect was only to have a large number of people on the verge of starvation instead of a small number."

No system of world government can possibly prevent wars of aggression if population pressures become intolerable. No scheme for sharing the wealth can mean much if there are more people than there is wealth to be shared.

What, to take a minor example, is the use of talking about "saving our National Parks" when it is perfectly obvious that there is no possibility of saving them if everything they contain, even the mere space they occupy, has become desperately needed?

The economists may tell us that only by a continuously increasing rate of population growth can prosperity be maintained, but the time must come when there is simply no room for any more people and long before that time arrives the problems created by overcrowding will be insoluble in any fashion compatible with an even moderately good life.

In many areas that time has already come, and there is even in America today hardly a plan to make human life safer or better either politically or socially which can be more than a temporary expedient unless somehow or other the mere number of men upon this earth keeps within reasonable limits. None of the major "world problems" is solvable on the assumption that population growth will continue at the present rate. On the other hand, a great many of them would not exist at all if, at the present moment, the population in many trouble spots were not too large for the physical or technical resources of the areas in question. Can there be any doubt that even in the United States, which is still, comparatively speaking, uncrowded, the rate at which the population is growing makes it very difficult to solve problems which would not otherwise be too difficult? Is is not, for example, the near impossibility of keeping up with growing needs which prevents us from remedying the much discussed inadequacies, physical and intellectual, of the educational system?

Why is it that most people still avert their eyes from this most fundamental of all world problems while they strive desperately for temporary amelioration? The very fact that no ready solution is available—not even a purely theoretical formulation which disregards all practical difficulties—is a partial explanation. But there never will be a radical solution unless the need for it is recognized, and the thesis here is (1) that the need is not adequately recognized and (2) that the reason is psychological as well as practical.

The most important practical problems have already been alluded to. On the one hand, prosperity as we know and worship it depends upon ever expanding consumption. Unless the "bumper crop of babies" grows larger and larger every year, not even the concept of "psychological obsolescence" plus the ever increasing demands of national defense can enable us to get rid of the goods we must produce if we are to continue to find employment for the men who operate machines whose productivity per man-hour continues to increase. On the other hand, should we find some way out of this dilemma we would still face the fact that if the population of other countries continued to increase we would al-

most certainly find ourselves someday invaded by hordes all
the more expendable because their own territories could no
longer support them.

Some realization of these stubborn facts reinforces a general unwillingness to contemplate the problems being created. But something else quite deep in human nature and
quite independent of rational argument complicates the situation still further.

Even those who have read the books and accept the figures resist the logical conclusion because that conclusion
outrages certain convictions which have roots so deep that
they penetrate into animal instinct itself. "Increase and
multiply" was a natural if not a divine injunction many millions of years before Genesis was written. The impulse to
multiply as rapidly and as profusely as possible is built into
the living organism. No animal before man ever opposed to
that instinct any prudential considerations relative to either
the parents or the offspring. To reproduce as multitudinously
as possible and to let nature deal as she may with the surplus
seems to have been the rule almost without exception. And
man himself responds to the ancient imperative far more
readily than to any which has been formulated during the
very brief period since the ancient injunction was even ten-
tatively qualified.

The chamber of commerce booster who takes it for granted
that his community is "progressive" just to the extent that it
is getting bigger, who assumes that all villages ought to become towns, that all towns ought to become cities, and that
the splendor of a city is measured by the urgency of its traffic problem has become a figure of fun to the intellectual.

But his premises are more ancient than theirs. When he cuts down the majestic elms which lined the village street to make way for the super highway and calls this "progress" his language may be vulgar but his instinct is of ancient lineage. And his premises are less different than some would like to think from the premises of those whose hearts rise at the thought that either their nation or some whole community of nations is "flourishing"—and who include as a necessary part of such flourishing getting bigger and more numerous.

In the days when it was still supposed that to make the techniques of birth control accessible would automatically reduce the birth rate, we used to laugh at the Catholic Church, which was accused of wanting more souls for heaven, at no matter what cost. But that its revulsion was far deeper than any theological apology for it is proved by the fact that most left-wing sociologists also refuse to consider population a problem and seem as eager to have more citizens for the proletarian utopia as the religious ever were to send more to their traditional heaven. In Latin countries they used to say, "God never sends a child without sending a loaf at the same time." Left-wingers have translated that dubious folk saying into an equally dubious sociological doctrine: technology always keeps pace with the needs of a growing population—or at least it would if the machinations of capitalist villains didn't prevent it from doing so.

Yet space, at least, would give out finally in the technologically most perfect world and there is no evidence that automatic checks operate soon enough anywhere "under the present system." The population continues to rise both in the United States where there is still abundance and in Puerto Rico where there is not. We are assured by what ought to be competent authority that even here our agricultural surpluses are certain to become deficiencies before long. And though it is all very well to talk about bringing the whole world up to our own level of plenty and comfort, verifiable figures demonstrate, as Harrison Brown has pointed out, that even the present populations of India and China alone could consume raw materials in excess of the world's present output. That output cannot possibly be extended indefinitely. There is a limit to the earth's resources and to our ability to exploit them. But there seems no limit to human fertility.

Such are the facts that only a few are willing to face, and they were not faced in most reviews of Harrison Brown's book because the reviewers, almost without exception, stressed what the author had to say about the problem of caring for an admittedly runaway population while paying little or no attention to his final conclusion, which was that these problems may be ultimately unsolvable. The plain truth seems to be, not only that we do not know what could be done to check the immoderate proliferation of the human species but also, what is worse, that we do not yet want to do anything about it; that we prefer to cling to the instinctive conviction that the more of us there are, the better. And we seem determined to continue to do so until one of three things happens: until war or pestilence wipes most of us out; until starvation removes a considerable though perhaps lesser number; or until, thanks to a technology which has advanced as rapidly as the most exuberant prophets predict that it will, we are literally living on top of one another in a world so intolerably crowded that even movement is almost impossible and we remain fixed to the supply lines of our cubicles like aphids on a rosebush.

One English engineer has seriously and happily predicted such a situation in a jaunty book called *What's the World Coming To?*, in which he cheerfully envisages apartment houses from which the inhabitants will seldom need to issue forth because nourishment will be piped in and social life will be conducted almost exclusively by way of private television sets. Nor is this vision as merely fantastic as one might suppose. Harrison Brown, drawing upon his astonishing mastery of geophysical data, expresses the belief that the earth could support in some fashion even the prodigious population with which it seems to be threatened—say fifty billion—under certain conditions; that it could support a hundred billion under certain other conditions; even two hundred billion under still others. And since demographers calculate that it will require several centuries at the present rate of increase to produce a population of even fifty billion, Mr. Brown seems to be giving us considerable leeway. But what are the conditions which would have to prevail?

Mr. Brown presumes not only the most successful imaginable technological advance but also, to provide for even the lowest of his three figures, the devotion of every foot of ground to immediately productive purposes. To double that figure we should have to depend almost exclusively upon tank-grown algae for food. To double it again we should have also to limit caloric requirements by severely restricting all movement not necessary to production.

Is it, then, any wonder that Brown should conclude by expressing his amazement that "A substantial fraction of humanity today is acting as though it were engaged in a contest to test nature's willingness to support humanity," and were determined not to rest content "until the earth is covered completely and to a considerable depth with a writhing mass of human beings much as a dead cow is covered with a pulsating mass of maggots."

At the present moment some men not only vaguely accept such a future but are actively and joyously preparing it. From time to time scientific journals report the progress of experiments in growing algae in sewage tanks and the process is now said to be practicable. Others, possessed of still bolder imaginations, expect even more of technology—as was recently illustrated in a statement by C. F. Kettering, of General Motors: "Despite today's farm surpluses, the human race must someday become independent of plant life . . . and that will be accomplished within the next fifty years." To Mr. Kettering, in other words, sewage-grown algae represented an unworthy compromise because it accepts as necessary the intervention of a natural process. When science has solved the mystery of photosynthesis it will have freed man from dependence upon any living thing other than himself. And when that day comes no inch of the earth's surface will have to be wasted upon any other form of life, plant or animal. All will be snuffed out and the globe covered with buildings as high as we care to make them.

In such a world the automobile will have of necessity disappeared, but Mr. Kettering no doubt consoled himself with the assurance that by then industrialists will be sufficiently busy with products not yet invented. And please notice that he said, not merely that the human race will, or could, or even should, become independent of plant life. He said that it "must" and he seemed to say it without regret. We cannot control population and, so he seemed to imply, there is no reason why we should want to.

Surely it is time to ask, not whether such a world as Mr. Brown describes with horror and Mr. Kettering seemed to contemplate with complacency, is possible, but also whether or not we want it. And if the answer is "no," then we should face the fact that unless we control population something like it is what we shall get—unless, that is to say, we get war, or famine, or pestilence first. One or all of them will be the penalty of our failure to develop a technology adequate to support an immoderate population. Mr. Kettering's world will be the reward—if reward is what we still insist upon calling it—of success!

If we really want a solution to the problem we may or may not find it. If we do not want a solution we certainly shall not. Yet it cannot, I think, be said that at the present moment most Americans, most Europeans, or most Asians do want it. And if the reason for that astounding fact really is that we are still too firmly in the grip of an instinct subhuman, subanthropoid, and submammalian, then we shall perhaps get nowhere until we realize that if we follow it blindly and indiscriminately we shall have to submit to one or another of nature's unpleasant methods of dealing with her surpluses.

· V ·

The Average and the Norm

An oculist who had the privilege of examining Bernard Shaw once told him that he had perfectly "normal" eyes. Mr. Shaw—being always Mr. Shaw—naturally told the world when the doctor added the cream of the jest: "A normal pair of eyes is one of the rarest things in nature."

For the first time, said Shaw, he realized why it was that whenever he announced some perfectly obvious truth he was accused of peddling fantastic paradox. His intelligence must be as normal as his eyesight. But because such normality is exceedingly rare he saw things in a fashion which the myopic, the astigmatic and the strabismic could not be expected to recognize.

One need not accept Shaw's own estimate of his intellectual equipment to see that the doctor's remark cut through a confusion in which psychologists and sociologists often flounder. Frequently they make no distinction between what is "normal" and what is "usual," "average," or "statistically probable." In fact they frequently deny that such a distinc-

75

tion can exist. To them there is not and cannot be any "norm" which is not merely an average. This is, indeed, the necessary conclusion of any thoroughgoing relativist.

If we follow their line of reasoning the phrase "a normal eye" ought to suggest, not an eye without refractive error, but one affected to an average degree by one or another of the usual defects. Or, to use a different example I once heard from Ralph Borsodi, the question "How many legs does a normal man have?" should be answered by finding a statistical average. And since some men have only one, or none, this would lead inevitably to the conclusion that a "normal" man is equipped with one and some fraction legs.

Unfortunately the results of this confusion are not always so merely comic. If to it you add the assumption that "normality" is the ideal to which both individuals and society should aspire the result is likely to be catastrophic. Since men "ought" to be normal and since the normal is the usual, one need only find out what men think, feel, and do in order to know what they *ought* to think, feel, and do; or, for that matter, just how intelligent, how selfish, how benevolent, and how conformist they *ought* to be. The most sensational recent example of this kind of reasoning is, of course, furnished by Dr. Kinsey's famous reports (or at least by the popular interpretation of them), which assume that to answer the question "To what extent is continence a virtue in either men or women, married or single?" all that is necessary is to find out what is the average number of extramarital sexual experiences each class has indulged in.

One need not put a very high value upon continence—in fact one might believe that contemporary society puts too high rather than too low a value upon it—to see that answering by statistics the question "How much *should* continence be valued?" is open to objection in its assumption that "normal" is average, that this sort of "normality" is desirable, and that, to repeat, one will know how men *ought* to behave if one can learn how, on the average, they *do*.

Less sensational examples of the same error may be even more important. There still is, after all, a strong conditioned —or perhaps humanly natural—resistance to extravagantly libertarian principles in the realm of sexual behavior. But there is much less check upon the "normal-equals-average" and the "average-equals-desirable" syllogism in other fields. Apply it, as many do, to every moral, sociological, intellectual, and artistic question and you get a society in which, metaphorically, any man who finds himself equipped with two complete legs is encouraged (or even required) to cut an inch or two off of one of them in order to achieve "normality."

A good deal has been written in recent years about the desire to "conform." But such criticism, like the criticism of Madison Avenue and "the hidden persuaders," is likely to be largely futile because it is concerned only with an isolated phenomenon and disregards the fundamental assumptions of even reputable philosophers, economists, and moral teachers on the basis of which conformity is as reasonable as the tendency of the advertiser to become the chief instrument of education. Just as you cannot object to the salesman as the hero most characteristic of our times unless you refuse to believe that increasing consumption is the greatest need of our civilization, so you cannot object to conformity unless you believe either that normality is undesirable or that it is not the same as average.

Perversely enough, advocates of nonconformity seem most often to dwell upon the neuroses and the self-destructive habits of distinguished men when they might make a more persuasive case if they would point out instead that a desire to rise above the average is at least as "normal" as a determination to rest in it.

If today we are obsessively concerned with statistical studies of the human condition, this is, of course, partly because we do attach enormous importance to "the average" as the most meaningful, the most instructive, and most useful measure of all things. But it is equally true that we prefer to believe this just because a statistical average is the kind of fact or "truth" which the techniques we have developed enable us to arrive at. We are committed to the scientific method and measurement is the foundation of that method; hence we are prone to assume that whatever is measurable must be significant and that whatever cannot be measured may as well be disregarded.

Thus the standard of living is measured because we think it is important. But it is also true that we think it important partly because we know that it can be measured. Thus also we consent to agree with Dr. Kinsey that a great stride toward the full understanding of man was made when he established what proportion of husbands and wives indulge in a given number of marital infidelities because we do believe this average to represent "normality." But we also tend to believe this to be true merely because his figures are the kind of facts we know how to get.

To an age which has mastered so successfully the techniques of measurement it is very reassuring to believe that whatever cannot be measured is identifiable with something which can be; or, in other words, that the standard of living is the same as the good life and that the statistics of extra-marital sex activity establish a norm defining for us a certain golden mean between debauchery and puritanism which we can safely assume to be the same thing as a virtuous life.

Similarly we can, for example, find out which activities teen-agers prefer, what courses of study they profess to find most interesting, and what books they read least unwillingly. Unless we do so identify the average with the normal and the normal with desirable we can only "discuss" rather than "establish" what constitutes good taste, rewarding activity, or the virtuous life. And a society wholeheartedly committed to the scientific method can hardly have much patience with what can only be discussed, never measured, demonstrated, or proved.

Nowhere are the results of these confusions more plain than in our conception of education. A former assumption was, not that it should be wholly a preparation for contented living on whatever level the world had sunk to, but that it was, in part at least, a deliberate attempt to criticize the prevailing condition of man and to create discontent with the kind of life which the average man lived. Since "average" had not yet been identified with "normal" and normal not yet accepted as defining all that is desirable, the educator could assume that part of his business was to foster aims, interests, ideals, and standards of value different from those which other strong social forces such as economic pressure and the inertia of the average human being tended to encourage. He assumed, in other words, that education

79

should exert an influence upon the human condition, not be merely a reflection of it.

Obviously such a conception is impossible on the basis of the premises now most widely accepted. It presupposed that the average is something to be risen above, not something to be clung to; that men can and should be better than they are; and that to find out what they prefer, know, and do is not necessarily to prove that this is all they should or can reasonably be expected to prefer, know or do. It assumed also that such things as superior knowledge, superior taste, and superior wisdom do exist and that teachers may be presumed more likely than their young charges to possess them. But because the "newer philosophy of education" refuses to make such assumptions, educators are now fanatically busy striking averages (which they call "establishing norms"), finding out what activities their charges prefer, and "preparing them for life"—which last means very much what the advertiser means when he speaks of his "educative function." In both cases what is meant is the attempt to persuade the entire population into an acceptance of the present condition of man as the most desirable which it is so far possible to attain and therefore one in which he should submerge himself as completely as he can.

More specifically, "establishing norms" means discovering what the average child has learned, how much he studies, and what tastes he has. And the purpose of establishing such norms is to make sure that no individual is required or even encouraged to rise above them. If a pupil does show more than average interest in "book learning" he is often suspected of being antisocial and advised to go out for basketball. If he is discovered to be reading books even slightly more mature than those assigned to his classmates he is often refused access to them and told that they are not suited to his "age group." Words which most children in any "age group" do not know are edited out of the texts given them on the assumption—or so it seems—that the chance that they might learn a few new ones is something to be carefully guarded against. The old saying that you do not know what you can do until you have tried, is indignantly rejected as likely to encourage "unreasonable demands" and what the child can and does do *without trying* is made the measure of reasonable expectation.

One great advantage to the professional educator of adopting these procedures is that they provide him with an almost impregnable bulwark against criticism. If any parents in city "A" complain that their children do not seem to be learning very much, then the authorities need only to reply: "The tests prove that the level of achievement" in reading, writing, and arithmetic is either equal to or even slightly above the "national average"—which is not so very surprising in view of the fact that it is just the "achievements" in this school and others like it which have established this average. And if the parents in city "B," where the schools are even a little worse, make a similar complaint then they can be assured that the level of their children's achievement is "almost as high as in city "A." Meanwhile the "norm" can be re-established and brought up to date from time to time so that it can sink lower and lower without anyone's being the wiser or feeling any cause for alarm.

The statement so commonly and so confidently made that education should be a "preparation for life" is meaningless unless the kind of life it is supposed to prepare for is specified at the same time. And if it turns out—as it usually does—to be the kind of life the average man now leads, then the aims of the educator and the advertising man are nearly identical and the senator previously quoted was entirely justified in inviting the latter to "participate more fully in the classroom situation." If the aim of the teacher is merely what anthropologists call "acculturation" then it is worth taking account of the fact that most children get much more of their education from advertisements, moving pictures, television, and popular songs than from school.

Critics sometimes complain that a considerable section of the curriculum in many state universities as well as in many high schools is neither "liberal" on the one hand nor "vocational" on the other, but merely trivial—as when for instance it is solemnly concerned with such topics as "movie appreciation," the points of etiquette involved in "going steady," the ethics of petting, and the aesthetics of the lipstick. Here, for instance, are statements which Professor Louise Pound has heard recently at educational conferences: "English should be a branch of social science"; "The main business of the English teacher is to teach citizenship"; "What have Shakespeare and Milton for the modern world?" Consider also the educational philosophy of a certain institution of "higher learning" which gives a course in "Telephone Techniques," described as including instruction in the art of beginning or ending a social conversation and in ordering groceries by 'phone.

Such courses are said to "prepare the student for life" as the reading of Shakespeare and Milton do not. And so, of course, they do if by "preparation for life" you mean simply and exclusively preparation for operating under the conditions which prevail among those who aspire to nothing beyond acceptance of their condition. There is no doubt that the average boy or girl actually is more interested in such things than in anything else. They do play a very important part in the life he leads and they are a genuine preparation for the life he will—if he is average—lead as "a well-adjusted adult."

Whereas the "normal" American never speaks of "professors," "academic learning," or even "the intellectual" except with contempt he is, nevertheless, very anxious to have his children go to college. And because our schools have fallen more and more into the hands of "normal Americans" they have eagerly helped him to escape from this dilemma. They have obligingly developed for him institutions of learning from which it is possible to graduate without having learned anything.

Such "courses of study" as the techniques of telephone conversation are grotesque only in the light of assumptions which the educators responsible for them do not make. The demands they make upon the student are those the "normal" student is prepared to meet. The topics dealt with are those in which he would, if queried, profess the liveliest interest; and they are a better preparation for the life he will probably lead than Plato, Shakespeare, or analytic geometry. The only thing to be said in favor of any of the latter is that they might possibly disqualify him for complete and contented immersion in the life of his times or even permit him to affect somewhat the future condition of man.

Thus that contempt for the intellectual of which some intellectuals complain is fostered by the members of what was once an intellectual group. There was a time when the common man had a perhaps exaggerated respect for "book learning" and supposed it to be the essence of education. Today, when some educators explicitly denounce "intellectualizing" as an evil tendency to be rooted out of the schools, he naturally despises what his mentors themselves despise.

The plight of the theoretical "educator" who has abandoned the hope or even the desire that education should guide or direct typifies the plight of the whole society of which he is a part. If he is now content merely to find out how children talk and to call that "acceptable English"; merely to find out what activities they spontaneously prefer and then to encourage them in those; merely to find out how much or how little they spontaneously learn and then to judge the "scholastic achievement" by that standard alone, it is because, like so many of his fellows among the students of adult society, he has renounced all belief in the legitimacy or the value of the attempt to say that the condition of man *should be* anything other than precisely what it is.

The United States Office of Education is now advocating what it calls "Life Adjustment Education" and the Educational Policies Commission of the National Education Association has recently proclaimed: "There is no aristocracy of 'subjects'. . . Mathematics and mechanics, art and agriculture, history and homemaking are all peers." But how could either consistently do otherwise unless it first broke with the fundamental assumptions of present-day society? To ask that education should criticize and perhaps seek to change the present condition of man instead of "adjusting" everyone to it is to ask it to assume the possibility that the human condition might be better than it is.

To ask the National Education Association to recognize some hierarchy of values is to ask it to do this and to do something else also, namely, to recognize the fact that there are definitions of "democracy" by which there is nothing necessarily "aristocratic" in believing that some "subjects" are more important than others and that an ignorant, uncultivated man is not necessarily in every respect the "peer" of an instructed and cultivated one. In the statement quoted above, the words "aristocracy" and "peer" are obviously loaded with an appeal to the prejudices of just that section of the public most deeply immersed in our present condition. Modern school men are very fond of reminding us that "education" means a drawing out, not a putting in. But was it ever before assumed that anything which could be "drawn out" was as valuable and as desirable as anything else?

Many of those who are busy implementing (if I may use one of their favorite words) the implications of the disastrously prevailing attitudes are probably incapable of understanding a criticism of it. They see nothing wrong with schools which do not lead their pupils but are led by them, or for that matter, with churches which join people instead of asking people to join them.

The more thoughtful who can and do understand the criticism will reply that though "ideals," "standards," and a "norm" may be theoretically desirable, we no longer believe that they are anywhere to be found and that those which, at one time or another, various civilizations did believe in and cherish were delusions which necessarily dissolved when the religious, or logical, or metaphysical systems which sanctioned them were exploded—as all such systems have been by modern rationalism and science. They were based upon faith in revelation or faith in the ability of the human reason to transcend rather than merely rationalize the condition of the reasoner, and it is by abandoning all such faiths that we have been able to achieve the advantages of that material wealth and powerful condition in which we now so happily find ourselves.

Perhaps a case better than any they have been willing to recognize could be made for the contention that at least some norm which is not merely an average could be defined clearly enough to be *usable,* and to that possibility we shall presently turn. But even if, as so many now confidently assert, *all* standards of value are arbitrary, it still remains true that any civilization which wishes to justify its boast that it is "controlling its destiny" must first choose, arbitrarily if necessary, the ends it is seeking. If it does not, then "control" is an empty word. Otherwise it can truthfully say only what in its franker moments ours does say: "We do not know where we are going; we do not know where we want to go; but we are on our way and we are doing everything possible to accelerate our movement." No civilization before ours ever traveled so fast either literally or metaphorically. Whatever the present condition of man may be, it is becoming daily more exuberantly and more extravagantly itself.

The church is the only other important institution which was traditionally on the side of the school and hence against "the world." It too stood for standards, ideals, and values which the world was prone to ignore. It too refused to regard the existing condition of man as constituting the norm of human life or to accept what men commonly did as defining what they should do. Hence it also could not assume that its chief function was to prepare all men for successful functioning in the world as it was. Like the school its aim was not to make men contented but to make them discontented. And just as the school regarded the average man as ignorant and vulgar, the church regarded him as wicked.

By our characteristic equation of "going to school" with "getting an education" we are now able to boast that ours is the best educated nation in the world. By assuming that "church membership" is proof of some sort of spirituality we have also convinced ourselves that we are in the midst of "a great religious revival." But churches, like schools, never before demanded so little—in the way of professed belief, unworldly ideals, or change of life—and the truth is not so much that "more people are joining the church" as that the church is joining more people. Just as those who have played football are supposed to be educated, so those who learn square dances or play bingo at the parish house are supposed to be religious.

"Attend the church of your choice," say the broadminded "church leaders"—which means, "Pick out the one which will confirm you in your beliefs, your aims, in your way of life." And of the millions who are accepting the invitation a very considerable proportion do so, not because they want or expect to be changed in any way, but only in the commonly gratified expectation that they will receive from one more institution the same assurance which they got from their schools, namely, that their present condition and the price they pay for it are worthy of praise.

Instead of expecting that some new truths will be brought home to them or that any new demands will be made, they are merely expressing their willingness to have the church bless whatever they do believe and do. If by any chance it fails to meet this expectation then it is obviously not "the church of their choice" and they will, of course, wisely choose another. Thus the church becomes one more sanction for the American Way, and though it to some extent does encourage the more amiable aspects of that way—its philanthropy and its concern for "welfare"—it has little tendency to suggest that this "way" might be transcended.

The most popular leaders of this strange religious revival are like most modern educators in that they dwell most insistently upon "adjustment" and "success." What they promise is, first, "peace of mind" and, second, "prosperity." One of the most influential sees nothing incongruous in illustrating the blessings of religion by assuring his readers that a jewelry salesman of his acquaintance sold more jewelry after he had "accepted Christ" than he had ever sold before. Nor does it seem to occur to him either that though "peace of mind" is desirable one may also ask how it is attained, or that "adjustment" may be considered an evil thing if it is an adjustment to evil.

Given these aspects of the present condition of man it is no wonder that there should have developed all those much-discussed phenomena called "conformity" and the "mass-man." Neither does there remain any basis for regarding them with disfavor.

Standardization has made the modern world and its high standard of living possible. If every automobile differed from every other they would be both prohibitively expensive to make and intolerably difficult to maintain or repair. Why should not men, like automobiles, be mass produced in the interests of efficiency? To that question there is no answer if the ideal man is the normal man and if the normal is the average man.

Because men still remain, despite all the increasing pressures upon them, to some extent variable and unpredictable, our law courts, our social service bureaus, even our psychiatrists' offices, have remained less efficient as repair shops than they might otherwise have been. But their tasks will be greatly facilitated as the machines with which they are called upon to tinker become less variable and more predictable than school, church, and society have so far succeeded in making them.

If not merely most men but all men wanted the same kind of house, enjoyed the same diversions and preferred the top tune on the Hit Parade to all other music, they could be both managed and catered to more successfully, and because the present wasteful consideration gives to various sufficiently large minorities would be no longer necessary, the majority could be provided with an even higher standard of living. The more machinelike a man is, the more easily he may be kept in good running order. Why bother with eccentric designs and obsolete models? They are no better than the standard and they are harder to service.

The negative answer we give to such questions was never more important. It only makes that much more effective the pressures and persuasions intended to win our consent; and they are more consistently manipulated than ever before. If men are nothing but the product of their society, if what is called "human nature" is actually determined by the existing system of production and distribution, then man will become more and more merely that creature whose desires and convictions and acts are best "adjusted" to his external condition.

If on the other hand, they are not "nothing but" the product of society, then to what extent can they refuse their consent to being molded by it? Do and can individuals differ in the ease and willingness with which they can be persuaded to give that consent?

We tend to answer such questions in the negative, not because we have considered them carefully, but because we yield to the pressure in that direction. If resistance is still possible it is more than usually difficult and it demands to an unusual degree the individual's faith in the reality and importance of his own individuality.

The very fact that men are so much more numerous than ever before tends in itself to make it more difficult for an individual to differ in any way from the other individuals who crowd in upon him. Of all the reasons which have been offered to explain why the mass-man should have emerged so conspicuously in our day, perhaps the most inclusive is simply the existence of a mass. The denser the population the closer and more continuous is the contact between man and man, the fewer the occasions when an individual is alone either physically or psychically, and the more difficult for him to lead any life which does not conform to the prevailing pattern. The more one sees of Mrs. Grundy (and the more she sees of us) the more attention we are inclined to pay to her disapproval. And in our present society she is less exclusively concerned than she used to be with morals, more concerned with all forms of eccentricity—including the failure to value most what our neighbors do.

In the realm of mere *things,* the near necessity of conforming is even more obvious than in the realm of tastes and opinions. The miracle of mass production which has made innumerable things cheaper than they ever were before (at least in the only meaningful sense, namely that they are within the reach of a larger proportion of the population) has at the same time made everything not mass produced more expensive, not only relatively but absolutely, and for the obvious reason that the price of labor is now based upon what a man plus a machine can make rather than upon what he could "custom make." Whatever millions do not want is a costlier luxury than ever before and within the reach of fewer and fewer people. That only a millionaire could afford a custom-built automobile does not matter. But it does matter that, for instance, space which was once cheap is now exceedingly dear and that it is now less expensive to live in the city than in the country just because the country is less completely mechanized. More and more people will be compelled to live close-packed whether they like it or not.

That all forms of popular education have come to rely upon machines confers upon popular culture the same advantages and the same limitations as those which characterize the mass production of things. The average man goes to a movie rather than to a play; listens to the radio rather than to a live concert; and, increasingly, to a radio or TV commentator instead of reading a newspaper. This means of course that the drama, the music, and the information are all mass produced and calculated for the common denominator of some very large group. One result is, notoriously, to make not only individuals but communities more and more alike, so that regional differences tend to disappear, and the "flavor" of a Maine village is less and less different from the flavor of a Texas town.

Moreover, any individual who does resist must resist more and more purely *as* an individual, because the very institutions—notably schools, colleges, and churches—which might be expected to encourage his refusal to consent are on the contrary increasingly devoted to the task of persuading him to accept his condition. In totalitarian countries uniformity is brutally imposed by the ruling class. Here it is achieved by a permissive method similar to that which proved so useful in providing a painless technique of exploitation.

Today the majority of even the more thoughtful have persuaded themselves while persuading others. If they feel somewhat uncomfortable in the position to which they are reduced, they feel bound to admit that they cannot see how "normal" can mean anything more than "average" or how any "standards" other than those which "the culture" provides could be established. The fact remains that when school and church alike take the average to be the desirable normal and assume that "acculturation" is the only defensible aim of education, it has become useless to protest against "conformity."

The words we choose to define or suggest what we believe to be important facts exert a very powerful influence upon civilization. A mere name can persuade us to approve or disapprove, as it does, for example, when we describe certain attitudes as "cynical" on the one hand or "realistic" on the other. No one wants to be "unrealistic" and no one wants to be "snarling." Therefore his attitude toward the thing described may very well depend upon which designation is current among his contemporaries; and the less critical his mind, the more influential the most commonly used vocabulary will be.

It is for this reason that, even as a mere verbal confusion, the use of "normal" to designate what ought to be called "average" is of tremendous importance and serves not only to indicate but actually to reinforce the belief that average ability, refinement, intellectuality, or even virtue is an ideal to be aimed at. Since we cannot do anything to the purpose until we think straight and since we cannot think straight without properly defined words it may be that the very first step toward an emancipation from the tyranny of "conformity" should be the attempt to substitute for "normal," as commonly used, a genuine synonym for "average."

Fortunately, such a genuine and familiar synonym does exist. That which is "average" is also properly described as "mediocre." And if we were accustomed to call the average man, not "the common man" or still less "the normal man," but "the mediocre man" we should not be so easily hypnotized into believing that mediocrity is an ideal to be aimed at.

A second step in the same direction would be to return to the word "normal" its original meaning. According to the Shorter Oxford Dictionary it derives from the Latin "norma," which has been Anglicized as "norm" and is, in turn, thus defined: "A rule or authoritative standard."

The adjective "normative" is not commonly misused—no doubt because it is not part of that "vocabulary of the average man" by which educators now set so much store. It still generally means "establishing a norm or standard." But "normal" seldom means, as it should, "corresponding to the standard by which a thing is to be judged." If it did, "a normal man" would again mean, not what the average man *is* but what, in its fullest significance, the word "man" should imply, even "what a man *ought* to be." And that is a very different thing from the "average" or "mediocre" man whom we have so perversely accustomed ourselves to regard as most worthy of admiration.

Only by defining and then attempting to reach up toward the "normal" as properly defined can a democratic society save itself from those defects which the enemies of democracy have always maintained were the necessary consequences of such a society. Until "preparation for life" rather than "familiarity with the best that has been thought and said" became the aim of education every schoolboy knew that Emerson had bid us hitch our wagons to a star. We now hitch them to a mediocrity instead.

Unless, then, normal is a useless and confusing synonym for average it should mean what the word normative suggests, namely, a *concept of what ought to be* rather than a *description of what is.*

It should mean what at times it has meant—the fullest possible realization of what the human being is capable of—the complete, not the aborted human being. It is an *entelechy*, not a mean; something excellent, not something mediocre; something rare, not common; not what the majority are, but what few, if any, actually measure up to.

Where, it will be asked, do we get this norm, upon what basis does it rest? Upon the answer to that question depends what a civilization will be like and especially in what direction it will move. At various times religion, philosophy, law, and custom have contributed to it in varying degrees. When none of these is available poetry and literature may do so. But unless we can say in one way or another, "I have some idea of what men ought to be as well as some knowledge of what they are," then civilization is lost.

·VI·

"Ideas Have Consequences"

No adequate description of the condition of man can confine itself to the material aspects of that condition no matter how broadly "material" may be defined. He leads his life surrounded, not only by things, but also by ideas and convictions. He acts, as has been shrewdly said, not upon the basis of facts but upon the basis of beliefs, even though the beliefs include "what he believes to be the facts."

Among the most important of his ideas, convictions, and beliefs are those which concern his own nature, his own powers, and the ultimate meaning or meaninglessness of his life. They constitute the intellectual and emotional atmosphere he breathes. What we think about ourselves is a significant aspect of our condition even if, as the most rigid expounders of dialectic materialism will insist, such ideas and convictions have no independent reality and exert no influence upon the material circumstances of which they are a mere by-product. At least they are part of the total environment.

Once a majority of the inhabitants of Europe and America professed to believe (and to some extent actually did believe) that they were the sons of God endowed with immortal souls destined for an individual existence throughout eternity; also that, at the center of each individual man, was a self-determining *persona* which could freely choose and act.

If this opinion was a true one, then it described the nature of man. If it was erroneous (as many scientists, many philosophers, and even many theologians have been tending to think), then this erroneous conception of man's nature and destiny was still a part of his condition though not, as he then supposed, of his nature. Any analysis of his present condition must ask for what truth (or what other error) he has exchanged it. What do men think about themselves today and to what extent are their thoughts significant aspects of their condition?

No doubt the most striking aspect of that condition is wealth and power; the next most striking, the readiness to accept this wealth and this power as the only measure of the satisfactoriness of their condition. But hardly less so than this flattering image is the low estimate man now has of *himself* —as distinguished from the wealth he possesses and the physical power he wields.

During the two centuries just past more and more human beings have become accustomed to doubt that they are the sons of God and that they have immortal souls. During almost as long a time great influence has been exerted by philosophers who hint or proclaim that the human being is not essentially different from the other animals and, what is even more important, that all animals are essentially machines whose behavior is not determined by the choices they are capable of making but by fixed responses to the stimuli to which they are exposed. Since this doctrine began to be widely preached the mechanists have greatly elaborated it without fundamentally changing its implications and they have succeeded in imposing it upon the majority of educated and thoughtful men.

Today the prevailing opinion among even the moderately intelligent and instructed is based largely upon their understanding and misunderstanding of Darwin, of Marx, of Freud, and, more especially, of their popular expositors. From the teaching of these masters they conclude: (1) that man is an animal; (2) that animals originated mechanically as the result of a mechanical or chemical accident; (3) that "the struggle for existence" and "natural selection" have made man the kind of animal he is; (4) that once he became man, his evolving social institutions gave him his wants, convictions, and standards of value; and (5) that his consciousness is not the self-awareness of a unified, autonomous *persona* but only a secondary phenomenon which half reveals and half conceals a psychic nature partly determined by society, partly by the experiences and traumas to which his organism has been exposed.

Thus though man has never before been so complacent about what he *has*, or so confident of his ability to *do* whatever he sets his mind upon, it is at the same time true that he never before accepted so low an estimate of what he *is*. That same scientific method which enabled him to create his wealth and to unleash the power he wields, has, he believes, enabled biology and psychology to explain him away—or at least to explain away whatever used to seem unique or even in any way mysterious.

Myths of his divine origin and of his immortality were exploded long ago without producing as much immediate effect as might have been expected. But much else has since been discarded almost as completely with more important consequences. The long effort to obey the injunction "Know Thyself" has to be abandoned, or at least reinterpreted. Man is now convinced that, in the sense intended, he has no self to know because he is only what circumstances have made him and because what it has made him is not a united "I" but only the shifting and dissolving configuration produced at a given moment by the interaction of his instincts, his reflexes, his complexes, and his traumas. Reason is but rationalization, choice but illusion, and standards of value but prejudices. And it was, so he believes, by admitting all this that he was enabled to achieve that power and that wealth which distinguish his present condition.

On the one hand he congratulates himself that he has ceased to be at the mercy of nature because he has learned her laws and can bend her to his will, making her serve *his* purposes, not hers. On the other hand he confesses that he himself is merely a part of nature and cannot be anything except what nature permits. He may boast of the power he has learned to wield and the wealth he has created but he must at the same time confess that he is himself the creature rather than the creator of the condition to which power and wealth have reduced him. He made the machine; but because the machine transformed society and he is necessarily the product of society, it is equally true that the ma-

chine is making him and that it will, in the future, remake
him into he knows not what.

His belief in his ability to *do* and *make* is greater than ever
before, even though, perhaps, it is so great as to suggest a
state of *hubris*. He has paid a strange penalty by feeling compelled to renounce even modest claims to any sort of *being*
for himself and to reach the conclusion that he cannot even
think except instrumentally and within the strict limits of a
rationalizing process which cannot define any ultimates or
criticize from any permanent center the convictions which
are the product of his environment. He regards himself as a
superb schemer, limitlessly ingenious in devising means, yet
so incapable of defining ends except in relation to means that
he must become the tool of his tools and confide his destiny
to the whims of developing technology. He is *Homo faber*,
not *Homo sapiens;* man the maker, not man the thinker. Thus
the great creator of machines comes to think of himself as
also a machine and though he continues to call himself "man
the maker" he can in actual fact see himself only as something which has, in its turn, been made. He is the great master of know-how but incapable of Reason or Wisdom. He
cannot control himself because he is inevitably what heredity
and environment have made him; he cannot choose good
rather than evil because the society in which he lives (perhaps, if he is Marxian, even the "instruments of production"
he has devised) determine what will seem good or evil.
Truly he is, for all his wealth and power, poor in spirit.

Sometimes he so far forgets himself as to talk wildly about
the need to "control our destiny" and about the prospect
that we shall soon be able to do so. What he seems to forget
is that "control" implies some defined end, a movement to-

ward some fixed point in the direction of which he wishes to move. But that is precisely what the dominant relativism cannot supply. You may call such a fixed point an "absolute," an "ideal," or even "a concept of the good life." You may even call it simply an accepted and acceptable "norm." But unless "norm" is somehow defined, we abandon the hope of "controlling our destiny" and are controlled by it instead—powerless to do more than to drift with the drift of our condition or, at most, to accelerate the developments arising from within it.

Of those aspects of man's condition which have to do with his estimate of his own nature and powers it is possible to give a documented description, though they cannot, like the economic aspects, be reduced to figures. Still other aspects, even less tangible, can only be inferred and the inferences are even more likely to be disputed than the best documented description of his self-estimate. Yet they are, for all, no less important aspects of his condition.

Perhaps the best clue—and we cannot get more than clues —is the key words which turn up most frequently in his discussions, arguments, and speculations, especially those large general words whose meanings in the particular context of the discourse are so much a matter of what they have come to suggest to those living at a given time and place that readers who come after often find vague or meaningless the very terms which, when they were spoken, seemed to indicate most clearly a universally recognized core of meaning.

Present-day scholars have filled books trying to explain to themselves and others what the eighteenth century can have meant by "right reason"—despite the fact that those who used it were right in their assumption that contemporary readers would suppose the meaning self-evident. Present-day critics are no less genuinely puzzled by what the Victorians meant to include in their so often invoked words "purity" and "impurity." Yet the preoccupation with "right reason" at one time and with "purity" at another is as significant for any attempt to estimate the condition of man during the eighteenth and nineteenth centuries as statistics describing per capita wealth would be in estimating his material condition.

What, then, are some of the key words which in the twentieth century correspond with these? The most obvious, of course, are "wealth," "power," "prosperity," "progress," and "welfare." This group reveals what we think we have achieved and relates to an aspect of our condition which we believe to be satisfactory. Hardly less obvious is another group composed of "adjustment," "security," and "peace of mind" which reveal quite as unmistakably what we feel still to be sought for. A less obvious but no less significant word which has been turning up with increasing frequency in discussions not concerned with measurable things is the richly ambiguous word "love."

There is, of course, nothing novel about the frequency with which the word itself is used. Unlike "progress," which is seldom met with in the modern sense before the seventeenth century, and unlike "welfare," "adjustment," and "security," which belong largely to the twentieth, "love" has, since at least the beginning of the Christian era, been used, analyzed, defined and celebrated more often than any other abstraction ever conceived by the human mind. Philosophers, moralists, poets, and theologians have spent a pro-

digious amount of time in praising or condemning it, and
especially in discriminating between the different kinds
which the use of one word for all has made so confusing.

But if there is nothing revealing about the difference between ourselves and our ancestors in the use of the word itself, a great deal can be inferred about our own or any other
time from the discriminations most often attempted and the
attitudes most often taken toward each of the varieties so
carefully and laboriously, if usually so unsatisfactorily, defined.

At one time the most important distinction was supposed
to be between the sacred and the profane; at another, more
tolerantly worldly, between the vulgar and the courtly. The
eighteenth century (still harping on "right reason") praised
especially "rational affection" and the nineteenth, of course,
not only thought the most important distinction to be that
between the pure and the impure but also was quite sure that
it could easily be made.

Perhaps, nevertheless, no century before the twentieth
ever found the subject quite so endlessly complicated or
spent quite so large a proportion of its time in discussing it.
To all the doubts, definitions, and discriminations inherited
from a past never entirely forgotten it has added all the new
facts and notions contributed by biology and psychology.
We have talked much about "the neurotic" as opposed to
"the normal"; and about "adjustment" as opposed to "in-
hibition." And yet, hard as we have tried, we have not quite
got rid of the sacred versus the profane or even the pure
versus the impure. Indeed, we had hardly achieved what we
believed a usable simplification by declaring that all love is
sexual love and sometimes avoiding the very word "love"

itself and using "libido" or "sex satisfaction" instead, when a new complication arose.

A decade ago you could be pretty sure that when the word "love" was used, sexual attraction of some sort was implied. It was very unlikely to mean, as in the past it very often did, *caritas,* and it was almost certain not to mean what used to be called "the Love of God." Today one cannot be quite sure. Only lurid paperbacks and pulp magazines now know merely one meaning of the word. If, for example, you see it in the quarterlies and then in one of the "home magazines" it is quite likely to mean two very different things. In the home magazines it most often refers to something which "children need" and which is defined as Tender Loving Care or, as the pediatricians now dub it, TLC. Elsewhere, however, as in the quarterlies, "love" very often means neither sexual desire nor TLC but something metaphysical and all but theological.

Psychiatrists speak highly of this last kind of love and sometimes say that neurosis (which used to be blamed largely on sexual prudishness) is most often both a manifestation and a cause of one of the key phrases of the moment, namely "the incapacity to love" in a special sense. What *this* kind of love "really is" is more and more discussed. It seems to include *caritas* but it is not simply that any more than *caritas* is merely what is meant by "charity" in the most limited sense.

Though as a people we are, or at least seem to be, almost obsessed with the desire to promote social justice, equality, and welfare, by the members of that minority which is seriously critical of man's present condition we are told that one of the characteristic and catastrophic deprivations from which contemporary man suffers is this same "inability to love." He has "satisfactory sex experiences"; he "gives his children love," even if he does not love them; and of course he promotes all sorts of causes calculated to promote "welfare" at home and abroad. Yet, so these critics suggest, there is a kind of love he is usually incapable of and without which sex experience, TLC, and a concern for the welfare of others are all as sounding brass.

Committed as the "normal" man now is to "realism" and "practicality," he will shrug off the distinction. Ideas, he will say, have no meaning, and emotions no justification except in so far as they result in action. If he has established "satisfactory sex relations" with his wife and if he "gives his children tender care," then he loves them all in every sense that matters. Anything else is shadowy, sentimental, perhaps even self-indulgent. He has heard more than enough of those who profess to be overflowing with love for everything and everybody without doing anything about it.

He is partly right. Though the special kind of love he most conspicuously lacks is not incompatible with Tender Loving Care, satisfactory sex experiences, and preoccupation with welfare, it does not always generate these good things as inevitably and as abundantly as perhaps it should. But it is nevertheless something very real. It is what the Ancient Mariner experienced when the ice went out of his soul because he had recognized that the water-snakes were beautiful and had "blessed them unaware." Its most obvious effects are the wonder and joy of the lover himself. He looks at the world he did not make and finds it somehow good.

To those who are incapable of this kind of love, nothing is beautiful. To those who are most fully possessed by it nothing is neutral, or commonplace or dull. Everything that is not evil and hideous is beautiful and good. They love themselves because they feel part of so many lovely things, while those who do not, in this sense, love themselves cannot love anyone or anything else.

Does not this definition suggest the true meaning of another key word often used by that minority which describes its dissatisfaction with the present condition of man as a sense of "alienation"? Though the "well-adjusted" citizen is often incapable of love he does not understand his state; those who are equally loveless but know that they are, properly call themselves "alienated"—not only from the well-adjusted individuals who surround them and the prosperous society of which they are a part but from what they believe human nature and the universe to be. They can love neither themselves nor anything not themselves. "Look you, this brave o'erhanging firmament, this majestical roof fretted with golden fire, why, it appears no other thing to me but a foul and pestilent congregation of vapours."

It cannot be that their alienation is an alienation from nothing more than the material condition of present-day man and from his acceptance of it. An individual might repudiate both yet remain at peace with himself and the universe. He can be alienated from them only if he finds the universe and himself incapable of inspiring love. At bottom, therefore, it is from himself that he is alienated and he is alienated because, having rejected the most obvious aspects of the present condition of man, he has not been able to reject also those convictions concerning the nature and the powers of the human being which are in part the cause and in part the consequence of the kind of society in which he finds himself. He cannot love himself because he has been convinced that man, though powerful, wealthy, and even well meaning, is neither admirable nor worthy of being loved.

Who or what has given him this low opinion of the species to which he belongs and from whose limitations he no longer believes it possible to free himself?

First of all it is, of course, that body of mechanistic, deterministic philosophy which has undertaken to deprive him of the power to choose, to rob him of the ability to reason, and to reduce his profoundest convictions concerning right and wrong to the status of mere cultural prejudices; which has taught him that he is not, that he cannot be, anything more than a product of conditions. But because these large philosophical generalizations remain remote and grand they are actually less immediately responsible for his sense of alienation than are the sociology and the sociological fiction which derive from them. It is from man as the novelists, playwrights, and poets have described him in detail and as the social worker has undertaken (often so successfully) to deal with him, that the imaginative inevitably feel most alienated.

Until comparatively recent times literature was the great secular force (more effective perhaps than religion and the church) which united men with one another by revealing to each the common ground of experience and aspiration on which they stood and, in this sense, reconciling the ways of God to man. It has never been easy for us to recognize ourselves in the abstract generalizations of the philosopher, the historian, or the scientist—not even when their intention was to be humanistic rather than antihuman. But the poet, the dramatist, and, sometimes, the novelist revealed more intimately than social life does how much we are like one another, how our secret thoughts are also the secret thoughts of others. In their works we recognized not only ourselves but our own image of ourselves, warm with emotion, capable of willing, thinking, and acting as we know from experience we do. They did not merely describe or explain the human condition as an abstraction. They communicated a recognizable image of it.

But since the mid-nineteenth century, more and more fiction in all its forms has become more and more subservient to scientific, sociological, and psychological theories; the writer seems less anxious to have us recognize ourselves than to make sure that what he writes could be taken to illustrate some scientific or sociological thesis he has accepted. At least from the time of George Eliot onward, many of the most important novelists tended to assume that fiction should illustrate "laws." Zola's endlessly reiterated thesis is that heredity and environment determine the character and the conduct of his characters, who are thus predictable products which circumstance has produced. Theodore Dreiser's *An American Tragedy* is another extreme example in which the hero is presented as in no sense a moral agent but again as only what he cannot help but be. Even where the thesis is less explicit, the tendency is very often to stress, not the individuality of the characters, but the extent to which they illustrate the "plight of the worker," the "limitations of the bourgeois mentality" or the "psychology of the postwar generation."

Thus literature has come to be a less and less effective corrective while the sociology upon which it leans so heavily becomes more and more drab as it more and more insolently disregards the intangibles and reduces human nature to the few crude needs, wants, and desires which it can recognize and measure.

It cannot, so it seems, give any account of either man or human life which does not leave out nearly everything which makes living interesting, enjoyable or significant. Though the Sociological Man is not quite so simple as that Economic Man who is nothing except producer and consumer, he is less likely to be recognized as a mere abstraction. If he is more than merely producer and consumer he is nevertheless motivated only by "needs," subject only to "pressures," desirous only of such unexalted goods as "security" and "status."

Even so relatively imaginative an economist as Veblen seems unable to resist the conclusion that the only "real" motives for human conduct are simple, crude, or unworthy and that the better he is understood the more evident it becomes that whatever seems to be inspired by subtler desires or to spring from worthier impulses is actually only the crude or unworthy in masquerade.

"Conspicuous consumption" is a telling phrase, though Veblen was by no means the first to observe that people sometimes spend money merely in order to call attention to the fact that they have it to spend. What was original in him was not the observation itself but the insistence that it provided a master key.

To say that when those who can afford it surround their

houses with a lawn it is because a lawn represents "uncon-sumed pasture" has, from the standpoint of the economist, the advantage of supplying an economic explanation for a characteristic bit of human behavior. It has also what he and the sociologists seem to regard as another advantage, namely, that of depriving man of one more example of what the naïve might suppose to be a love of the beautiful for its own sake. But is the explanation generally or universally true? "He that has built for use, till use is supplied must begin to build for vanity," wrote Samuel Johnson, and that remark is sufficient proof that "conspicuous consumption" is not a new conception. But Johnson would never have assumed that the beauty of a lawn was not part of "use."

That lawns can be used merely to demonstrate how much luxurious display the owner can afford is obvious. Good food is sometimes served at table and good pictures are sometimes hung on walls for the same reason. But it is no more true to say that the only possible meaning of good food or great art is the conspicuous consumption they may involve than it is to say that lawns are never cultivated except for the same rea-son. There are men who enjoy good food even in private, who are genuinely moved by great art, and who maintain lawns because they give pleasure to the eye. But these are motives in which, for some reason, the sociologist is unwilling to be-lieve. And just because he does dismiss as unreal the best mo-tives of the best men his account of human behavior becomes a libel on the human race and makes man a singularly dull as well as unattractive animal. Hamlet's "What a piece of work is man!" tends to become instead, *"What* a piece of work is man!" Perhaps we can still desire his welfare. Perhaps we can still "give love" and TLC to the child inevitably destined to become such a man. But can we possibly love either in the different and fuller sense?

From time to time sociology brings into prominence some new or at least newly emphasized "pressure" or "drive," though it is rarely if ever one which contributes anything to man's dignity or worthiness. "Conspicuous consumption" seems to have had its day, and at the moment "the desire for status" is enjoying a great vogue.

Under this designation is lumped without discrimination any aspiration toward distinction of any kind. "Garbage collectors who pull political wires to get themselves appointed manager of the city dump" (the phrase is H. L. Mencken's) are men seeking status; so is anyone who aspires to recognized excellence or eminence in any field of human activity. To make any distinction would be to deal in intangibles, and intangibles are abhorred by science.

Moreover, the word "status" is seldom used without at least faintly derogatory connotations. It always seems to imply a mean desire to justify the feeling that one is better than one's neighbors; and the implication seems to be that if the desire for status (which includes all the various not quite identical impulses which used to be called "ambition," "aspiration," "pursuit of excellence," et cetera) could somehow be eliminated, we should be a great deal nearer to the achievement of that true democracy in which all real as well as all artificial distinctions have been abolished. Then all men would have not only equal opportunities (which constitutes the first step) and be equally secure (the second step) but would also be and remain in every respect equal. The very concept of status will have to disappear in a truly class-less society—which means of course that every desire to *know* more, *do* more, or *be* more than the average will have to disappear along with the commoner desire to *have* more.

The distinction between ambition (which is the *last* infirmity of noble minds) and aspiration (which is not an infirmity at all) may be even more difficult to define securely than the difference between hoping that one will be recognized as a great poet and pulling political wires to get oneself appointed manager of the city dump. But it is just because sociology cannot make the distinction and literature can, that literature gives the truer and, ultimately, the more useful account of human life. In the sociological man hardly more than in the economic man do I recognize myself, my friends, or even, for that matter, such sociologists as have come under my observation. It is not what we are like because, at a minimum, it is not what we seem to ourselves to be, and what we seem to ourselves to be has a great deal to do with what we are.

These really are confused and troubled times. Perhaps the world has seldom been so puzzling and so insecure. But it has often been very strikingly so without, in so far as we can judge, producing an epidemic sense of "alienation." Perhaps what so many now feel alienated by and from is not man or society but the picture of both which sociology and psychology offer and which has been increasingly accepted as the truest picture. How can anyone who truly believes that his fellow man is nothing but the sociological man "subject to pressures" and that his mental and emotional life can be adequately described in terms of his "sex satisfactions," his impulse toward "conspicuous consumption" and his "desire for status," possibly feel anything other than alien to him?

No doubt it has always been true that the intellectual and the artist have been more likely than other men to reject the standards of their society and even, in extreme cases, to approach that total rejection of man which we have been calling "alienation." But there have been few previous periods in history when so large a proportion of the talented and esteemed artists in music and the graphic arts as well as in literature were so obviously as they now are what the young English writer Colin Wilson called "Outsiders"—meaning, most inclusively, simply "at outs" with their fellow citizens. At its plainest and simplest their rejection is merely a protest against getting and spending as the be-all and end-all of human life and they find it no more acceptable when it is renamed "production" and "distribution." In its more extreme form it is either total alienation or that escape from alienation which the mystic achieves when he has reached the conviction that by total alienation from the visible and tangible world he has made contact with a supersensual reality to which he "belongs" as obviously as he is alien to the other.

The worldling has always existed side by side both with mystic and with those who, without being mystical, have to some extent rejected the world as they find it. But there is significance in the fact that in this, the richest, most prosperous, and, seemingly, most comfortable civilization which ever existed, the artists in all media should be so consistently in opposition to the average citizen whose absorption in the goods his world supplies him with is even less tempered than it usually has been by some concern, religious or other, with intangibles.

Even most of those who are neither Christian nor, in any ordinary sense, mystical do nevertheless feel that there is something lacking in our society and that this lack is not generally acknowledged; do feel that, for all its prosperity and for all its kindliness, generosity, and good will, it is somehow shallow and vulgar; that the vulgarity is superficially evidenced in the tawdriness, the lack of dignity and permanence in the material surroundings of our lives, and more importantly in our aims and standards; that we lack any sense that efficient and equitable systems of production and distribution are only a beginning, as, for that matter, are also our ideal of democracy and our struggle for social justice. You may, as a few do, attribute this alienation to "a lack of religion." But perhaps even that term is not broad enough. It is a lack of any sense of what life is *for* beyond comfort and security, and it would still be so even if all these good things were conferred upon all. At best life would still remain, in Yeats' phrase, "an immense preparation for something which never happens."

·VII·

The Failure of Attention

Neither the critics nor the proponents of the welfare state
have concerned themselves much with the definition of "welfare." In what does it consist and how much does it include?
Is it something to be granted or something to be imposed?
Does it, in other words, mean giving people what they want
or what someone thinks they ought to have?

If it means the former, then which wants of which people
come first? If it means the latter, then by what criteria can a
relativist society judge "what they ought to have"?

One answer to these usually neglected questions is given
by David Thomson, lecturer in history at Cambridge University and author of *Europe Since Napoleon: World History
from 1914 to 1950.* Though apparently a staunch propo-
nent of the welfare state, he writes as follows in an article
called "Basis for a New Political Philosophy," published in
the New York *Nation* in 1957:

"The Welfare State . . . exists to provide whatever the

community regards as beneficial and good. If the community regards automobiles, TV sets and football pools as of greater value than better schools, more generous care of old people and a creative use of leisure, then the democratic state will provide more automobiles, TV sets and football pools."

Mr. Thomson certainly gives the impression that he has preferences of his own and that they are not what he believes to be those of most people. But he does not appear to have tongue in cheek when he yields to the only definitions of "democracy" and "welfare" which his relativist philosophy afford him. Like most of our contemporaries he is unwilling to consider the possibility that "what the community regards as valuable" is not the only possible standard by which values may be judged. Nothing is better than anything else except in so far as it gets more votes. Thus democracy is defended, not because of any conviction that its decisions are on the whole wiser than those of other governments by some independent standard but simply because *any* decision which has majority sanction is "wise" and "right" by the only possible definitions of those terms. If the normal is only the average; if the good life is whatever the majority thinks (or has been persuaded to think) that it is; if what men *should do* is whatever they *do do;* then it must follow that the desirable is whatever is most widely desired and that "democracy" means that what the majority admires is excellence. Mr. Thomson himself may prefer "a creative use of leisure" to football pools, but he is too broad-minded to suppose that such a preference is more than one of those tastes about which there is no disputing.

Laissez faire is generally supposed to describe the social

theory diametrically opposed to that of the welfare state, but here one sort of laissez faire is exchanged for another. Though the economy is to be "planned," society is to be allowed to drift, intellectually and culturally, with the economic and technological currents.

Under democracy of the older sort the most fundamental right of the citizen was assumed to be the *pursuit* of *happiness*. The welfare state substitutes "welfare" (definable in material terms) for "happiness" and then, by way of compensation, assures him that his right is to the *attainment* rather than merely to the *pursuit* of this supreme good. But though we may "pursue" whatever kind of happiness seems to us most worth pursuing, the "welfare" assured us must be mass produced, whether it is (as under dictatorships) defined as what the dictator thinks we ought to have or (as in our society) as what the majority has been persuaded it wants.

The nearer the welfare state comes to achieving its ideal, the less likely it becomes that happiness can be achieved by anyone whose conception of it does not coincide with that of the majority. If soap operas are what he wants he will surely get them. If he is pursuing happiness in some less popular form his chance of catching up with it seems less good. "You don't care for football pools?" Well, as the old joke had it, "Comes the revolution and you will."

Liberals have never been more concerned than they are today about "minority rights"—provided the minorities are national, racial, religious, or political. But they have seldom shown less concern for those minority rights which are intellectual, cultural, or temperamental. The individuals who make up minorities of this second sort are more likely to be dismissed as maladjusted, and the only right the maladjusted have is the right to such help as school, church, and social service can give them in achieving "normality."

It seems generally assumed that the opposite of "totalitarian" is "democratic." In actual fact neither the words themselves nor the realities to which they correspond stand in any such relationship. "Totalitarian" means a government so unified, centralized, concentrated, and consistent that there can be no conflict of powers or principles, no possibility that either individual citizens or such different components of the social structure as school, church, industry, etc., can pursue different goals or be governed by different ideals. Hence the opposite of "totalitarian" is not "democratic" but "pluralistic"; and a democracy may, in theory at least, be either the one or the other.

So far no democracy has become clearly totalitarian, but there is no theoretical reason why the will of the majority expressed through the ballot box might not impose any or all of the restrictions and uniformities enforced in Nazi Germany or Communist Russia. Only in so far as it "respects minority rights" and to that extent mitigates complete subservience to the "will of the majority" does a democracy resist the totalitarian implications of the simple phrase "majority rule." In the long run, "minority rights" are not likely to be protected by anyone except the members of the minority itself, and they have less and less power to protect those rights as majority desires and tastes are more and more accepted as themselves establishing all ultimate value judgments.

No doubt the example of the totalitarian dictatorship has

made it even less likely than before that our own democracy will go as far in the totalitarian direction as a Senator McCarthy, for example, would have liked it to go.

But we have no such cautionary examples of that milder social and cultural totalitarianism which is now so commonly noted under the name of "conformity." The exigencies of mass production automatically encourage it because, as a Marxian might say, we must conform to the logic of our system of production by all buying the same goods. It is also encouraged philosophically by the assumption that—as Mr. Thomson put it—the duty of the welfare state to give the community what it wants means in effect that *all* must take what the *majority* want.

Pluralism implies, for example, that independent enterprises offer soap operas on the one hand and literary drama on the other. At its logical extreme the welfare state would discover which the greatest number of its citizens wanted, tax everybody to support that, and then offer it free as a social service. In so far as we drift in the direction of that logical extreme, just to that extent do we approach cultural totalitarianism. At the present moment there are, for example, tax-supported golf courses for which everyone must pay, thus leaving the non-golfers that much less with which to buy tickets to the symphony which is not tax supported because the majority does not want it.

Just how much further we are likely to go in that direction is certainly an open question. On the other hand it does seem beyond dispute that the more intellectual members of the community have less influence than they once had upon, say, what the schools shall teach and also that they have come to receive a smaller and smaller share of the tangible benefits conferred by the condition called prosperity.

Opponents of a thoroughgoing egalitarianism have always maintained that "leveling" inevitably meant "leveling down." Defenders of it have always denied this generalization and today they are likely to point out that though communism does seem to level down, democracy in the United States has leveled up and is, in fact, tending toward the complete abolition of any class of the dispossessed and exploited. Communism, so they say, may make everyone a proletarian but American democracy has all but eliminated proletarianism. And they like to believe that though the overprivileged may have been quite properly deprived of some of the privileges of their position there is no other class which has not shared in the "rising standard of living."

Yet in respect to one group at least this is demonstrably untrue. The college professor, far from participating in the increased national income, has found his "real wages" and his "standard of living" declining sharply—not only relatively but absolutely—so that he has less rather than more than a decade or two decades ago. In this case at least our society has said, "From him that hath not shall be taken away."

To what extent other members of the intellectual class have suffered the same fate as the college professor it is not easy to say, but so far as the professor himself is concerned, the decline of his "standard of living" is not a matter of mere general impression but can be clearly read in the only light we trust today, the light of statistical tables. According to a study made by the Ford Foundation the average real income of the factory worker rose 43 percent between 1943 and 1953 while the average real income of the full professors at 120 state universities was 24 percent *less* in 1953 than it had been in 1939. Nearly everyone agrees that the factory worker's income should have risen. Some may maintain that the college professor's was high enough already. But few would say that it should have declined sharply while that of almost all nonintellectual workers was rapidly rising.

Why then did it do so in a society which boasts that it is "planned"? Was it because of a general contempt for the intellectual?

To that question the answer probably is, "Only in small part if at all." The most important fact is that the professor is a member of a class too small either to exercise direct political power or to count in the calculations of the planners. The income of the factory worker rose, not only because he was in a position to demand that it should, but also because the majority of even those who had no philanthropic commitment to him accepted the prevailing economic philosophy which holds that because "adequate purchasing power" alone can preserve prosperity, high wages are a benefit to the capitalist as well as to the wage earner. But underpaid college professors are not numerous enough to constitute a threat to the economy no matter how hard they work or how little they consume. Just as their influence at the polls is too slight to put any effective pressure upon politicians, so their involuntary effect upon the level of consumption is too slight to concern even the most disinterested "planners." If they were as numerous as farmers there would be great concern over their failure to get "a fair share of the national income." But they aren't.

Almost as striking is the professor's failure to participate in the second great boon—leisure. He has less and less time for either contemplation or research. His classes get larger; his obligations to advise, counsel, or generally comfort individuals and to sponsor student activities become more and more burdensome. He is also more and more likely to have to teach summer school if ends are going to meet. No matter how much leisure the machine may have created, he, at least, doesn't seem to get any of it. And if it were not that the foundations (which are among the characteristic institutions of a pluralistic society) enable him to snatch a year now and then, he would have precious little chance of demonstrating that "productivity" which his institution demands but certainly doesn't provide time for.

Moreover, this failure to win leisure is one which he shares with those intellectual workers whose wages have, unlike his, risen. There is, indeed, a stubborn fact which tends to prevent a fair share of leisure from going to anyone whose work depends upon any skill, knowledge, or capacity not so clearly definable and so readily available that he may quit when the whistle blows and turn his job over to someone else who can take it up just where he left off.

Neither the mass production of goods nor the invention of labor-saving devices has made the job of being President of the United States any more leisurely. In industry itself, the big executive is not enjoying a shorter work week. The usual week of the statesman, the executive, and the research scientist cannot be shortened by dividing it into three shifts.

If by leisure you mean what Thoreau called "a margin around my life"; if you mean, that is to say, waking hours which can be devoted to pursuits not connected with the making of a living, then it is obvious that already, even when, as many think, the era of high wages and short hours has just opened, the industrial worker in one of the large industries has more leisure than either his boss or most of those engaged in those occupations where the individuality of the worker has an important bearing on his job. Business executives, successful doctors, and successful lawyers—unlike research scientists and professors—make more money than factory workers. But they have less leisure.

Briefly and very early in his career, Thoreau was half-convinced by a crank named Etzler, who was one of the early proponents of the theory that the result of improved technology should—and ultimately would—be not an increase in material goods, but an increase in the leisure which, of course, the average man was going to use in the pursuit of wisdom and beauty. Bernard Shaw was one of the moderns who followed this same line and professed to see just ahead the time when two or three hours of "robot labor" a day spent in some such "brainless occupations as machine tending" would support a population of artists and philosophers. But the catch seems to be that even in the most thoroughly mechanized society there will still be a lot of brain work to be done, and that those who have the brains to do it will be the very ones who cannot knock off after two or three hours. While the amount of manual work necessary to keep our society going grows less and less, the amount of thinking which has to be done grows greater and greater. No doubt the job of the intellectual worker is more interesting and it is sometimes urged that, for that reason, he neither needs nor wants leisure. But he does need wide interests and wide knowledge. It used to be said that the pure specialist was pure idiot and we are beginning to realize what it would mean to be ruled by experts who had no wide grasp of anything. But the specialist is, nevertheless, being compelled to specialize more and more intensely—presumably becoming in the process more and more of an idiot.

Perhaps, as some say, that situation is so new that no hasty conclusion concerning its ultimate results should be drawn. Though we may seem to be taking leisure away from those who could use it and bestowing it upon those for whom "entertainment" has to be provided, education and opportunity will correct the unfortunate condition. Another generation born to leisure and a high standard of living will, it is sometimes argued, take better advantage of them and the "worker" who works only four hours a day for three days a week will learn to read, think, create, and contemplate. He will be a member of a new leisure class more valuable than any previous elite because it will constitute a majority rather than a minority and because it will no longer be parasitic.

That day is at least not yet arrived. The intelligent and educated man seems to have less and less time to read books, think thoughts, or enjoy the arts while the manual laborer has more and more time which he seems incapable of disposing of unless stultified by one or another of the mass entertainments. Those who purvey these last can hardly be expected to undertake the task of weaning him away from them, nor does that economic philosophy which holds that increasing consumption is the key to well-being give any encouragement to those who would. "Cultural activities" are nearly useless under an economy of abundance because they use up little or nothing. "Highbrows" spend too much time reading the same old books, looking at the same old pictures or even, God save the mark, in "contemplation." But the mass-man's diversion always involves expenditure. The more leisure he has the more TV tubes are worn out, and the more crooners are given employment.

To all this "education" is supposed to be the answer. The proper and fruitful use of leisure was, it is true, once supposed to be one of the things which education undertook to teach. Now it is less and less inclined to attempt anything of the sort. The typical attitude is that revealed in the report of a New York State committee which advises that, since the so-called classic literature is disliked by present-day children and does not mean anything to them, it should be dropped from the schools in favor of easier reading matter. Some may think that the business of education is to see to it that the best that has been thought and said is meaningful rather than meaningless to those who have been schooled, but the current assumption is that the school should merely make more accessible what the uneducated can already understand without effort.

If, as the National Education Association proclaimed, "there is no hierarchy of subjects" and "mathematics and mechanics are peers" there is also no hierarchy of leisure occupations. Reading *Hamlet* may be admitted to be the "peer" of watching a wrestling match on the television screen but it is no more than a peer. One survey made by the Gallup Poll may reveal that 61 percent of all adults could not remember having read one book during the year just passed and that 26 percent of college graduates were in the same position. Another long-term study conducted by the firm of Cunningham and Walsh may reveal that in a typical community the average time spent on *weekdays* before the TV set is three hours and twenty-one minutes while only 50 percent of the adults devoted any of their evening time even to magazine reading. (Presumably it was statistically not even worth inquiring about books.) But if average is normal and normality is desirable, then the only citizens whose habits should be regarded as open to criticism are those who do *not* spend three hours and twenty-one minutes per weekday looking at a television screen.

Still, these studies certainly do dispose of two myths—the myth that "almost universal schooling" is producing a population educated in any of the conventional sense of the term and the myth that the small doses of "culture" disseminated through the mass media are leading the members of the mass audience to richer pastures. And if by any chance it is not true either pragmatically or metaphysically that all subjects of study and all leisure occupations are peers then the present situation is not one in which it is possible to take much satisfaction.

If it is not true metaphysically, if the recognition of a hierarchy of values is indispensable to any good life, then we are not leading one. If it is not true pragmatically, if the stability of our society depends upon our learning certain things and developing certain habits of mind, then the principle of laissez faire in education may be as much of a threat to the continuance of democratic society as laissez faire economics is generally supposed to have been.

Something in the American temperament as well as in the relativist philosophy predisposes us to an intellectual and cultural laissez faire. Thus our admirable kindliness has its less admirable aspect since we are also what may best be de-

cribed as "easygoing"—so easygoing that we hesitate even
o encourage, much less to enforce, discipline or to encour-
ge, much less demand, effort, at least in intellectual or cul-
ural matters. It used to be believed that freedom, to be prof-
table, presupposed a disciplined preparation for it. Now it
begins, literally, in the cradle. The infant is raised "permis-
sively"; the child chooses his own occupations; the adolescent follows his impulses. If the child finds comic books eas-
er than real books, if the adolescent prefers rock and roll to
music and the adult soap operas to drama, then let them
have them. Why not, if it makes everybody happy? No doubt
it is the social duty of advertisers to persuade everyone to demand the best (even if it is only a "psychological" best) because prosperity depends upon consumption. But vulgar
taste in the arts is not going to reduce anyone's "standard of
living" no matter how prevalent it may be.

An earlier American may have been too much inclined to
believe in all work and no play. In his day he was accused
of holding "cultural" and "intellectual" pursuits in small
esteem because they served no utilitarian purpose. But it is
certainly not true that his descendent believes in work only,
either for himself or for others. As a matter of fact, "recreation" is almost an obsession. Insufficient opportunities for it
are commonly held responsible for a wide variety of social
problems. "Recreational facilities" are a principal concern of
municipal authorities and—so at least it sometimes seems—
the principal concern of public schools. But if the typical
American no longer believes in work only, he now seems to
believe so firmly in nothing but work *and* "recreation" that
he is hardly aware of anything which is not the one or the
other. Thus the boy who divides his time between the books

he hates and the games, dances, etc., he loves becomes father
to a man who divides his between "work" in office or shop
and "recreation" on the golf course or at the wrestling match.

Yet only in a barbarous society is it true that all valued activities are either utilitarian or recreational. A large proportion of those activities which are civilized and civilizing do
not belong under either head. Certainly the deepest satisfactions which art, science, and literature can yield come when
we are neither trying to use them for any practical purpose
nor merely "recreating" ourselves, but rather when we have
entered into some relationship too strenuous to be mere recreation, too immediately rewarding not to be cultivated for
its own sake. To a lesser degree, most of what are called hobbies partake of the same character, whether they be photog-
raphy, amateur dramatics, or birdwatching. And though it
cannot be said that Americans do not cultivate many hobbies
it is obvious nevertheless that the "facilities" to which state
and school devote so much attention are mostly for mere recreation, to a much smaller extent for creative hobbies, and almost not at all calculated to encourage the most civilized
and civilizing activities. All work and recreation makes Jack
a well-rounded barbarian—which seems to be what many
mean by "a healthy, normal, well-adjusted American."

In certain respects we are no doubt still a strenuous people, but we do not lead and we do not believe in the benefits
of a strenuous intellectual life. What we find most admirable in radio and television is that they make what they have
to offer so accessible; in our periodicals that there are no long
solid blocks of text that have to be plowed through; in modern methods of education that they are so painless and easy.

The Failure of Attention

Everything seems designed to be glanced at rather than attended to, as though "labor saving" were desirable mentally as well as physically. If the telephone which can be answered without having to lift a receiver represents one ideal, the book that does not really have to be read is another.

Some years ago Mr. Clifton Fadiman used—and for all I know may have invented—the phrase "the failure of attention." Nearly everyone seemed to recognize its aptness. It covered everything from the schoolteachers' complaint that children would no longer take the trouble to learn arithmetic, to the publishers' discovery that "condensations" sold better than original masterpieces and that pictures which could be glanced at were increasingly preferred to essays which had to be read.

The college student plays the radio while he studies because he cannot keep his mind on his books; vacationers at the beach take along a phonograph, a deck of cards, and various other pieces of paraphernalia because neither the sea itself nor any one of their other diversions can hold them for long. Even the magazines which professedly address the more intellectual audiences find it continually necessary to become more "striking." The newspapers' discovery that bigger headlines paid off was followed by the magazines' discovery that only an arresting make-up would enable them to survive. No one can be expected any longer to open a monthly simply because he has learned from experience that it will contain something interesting. His attention has to be caught by a snappy title, a striking picture, a teasing promise held out. Even among more intelligent and better educated people it can no longer be assumed that they will *give* their attention. It has to be *caught*.

Some who are mildly disturbed by these phenomena explain them by saying rather sourly that we all "have too much," and that we are like a spoiled child who can never be entertained because he has too many toys. Others, refusing to be disturbed at all, explain rather complacently that ours is merely a world which is richer, livelier, and more vivid than it used to be. But is it? Does a child who comes home from a school where he has had his "natural interests" nervously catered to, who then goes out to the movies and comes home again to a television set (this is precisely the usual routine of my friends' children) really lead a richer life than the nineteenth-century child who had nothing arranged for his entertainment after school and was therefore encouraged to be active instead of passive—to read, build, collect, or play a musical instrument instead of allowing himself to be force-fed by "sponsors" with something to sell. Does the adult who glances through a picture magazine, skims a news weekly, watches ten minutes of a Senate investigation on TV, and then hears the scherzo movement of a symphony on the "Ford Hour" really live a richer life than his grandfather who actually read the *Atlantic Monthly?* It is not what you have available but what you take in that counts. And there are a great many adults, as well as a great many children, who don't seem to have time to take anything in.

Recent advertisements of a well-known encyclopedia make their pitch on the number of illustrations which that still valuable work contains and on the fact that it is "as interesting as a picture magazine." Perhaps it is. But that is not the most important thing about it. What is the condition of a public which buys an encyclopedia, not because it is full, accurate, and authoritative, but because it is "as interesting as a picture magazine"? It is more expensive than a picture magazine and to buy it for the pictures is a waste of money. Is an encyclopedia wise to enter into such competition on such terms? If the answer is that it cannot do otherwise, that no sufficient public will buy it on the basis of any more substantial claims, then will it not inevitably find it more profitable to become more and more completely no more than a permanently bound set of picture magazines? And if that is what encyclopedias cannot help becoming, should colleges compete with television on approximately the same level? Or should colleges and encyclopedias alike assume that they exist for some audience (small though it may be) that demands something which only colleges and encyclopedias can give. Is a devotion to "democratic principles" a danger to democracy itself if it leads to a neglect of those who are willing to seek out rather than merely to accept whatever is most accessible, to give their attention rather than wait to see who will capture it, to make the effort necessary to comprehend what cannot be made comprehensible at a glance?

Never has there been more talk about "communication"—about "methods of communication," "the need for communication," and, alas, "the failure of communication." There are, so we are told, urgent reasons for all this. Never before were there so many things which the world needed to know. Never before was it so important that everybody should understand what was once the business of "the ruling class" alone. Educators and publicists must study "mass communication" so they can reach the common man. But is the acknowledged "failure of communication" the result of defective methods and to be remedied by devising better ones, or is it the re-

sult of a failure of attention on the part of those addressed
which further simplification will only encourage? Should the
child who cannot and the adult who will not read be given a
picture to look at instead? Or will that only make them less
and less capable of reading?

Are what our school principals grandly call "audio-visual
aids" usually anything more than concessions to the pupils'
unwillingness to make that effort of attention necessary to
read a text or listen to a teacher's exposition? Can anything
be said in favor of most of them except that they are, at best,
a surrender to the delusion shared by children and adults
alike that the mechanical techniques of communication are
interesting in themselves, no matter what (even if it happens
to be genuine information) is being communicated? Are they
not, at worst, merely devices for "catching" an attention
which can never be given freely or held for long? How often
can it be said that any movie, film strip, or recording teaches
the so-called student—who has dwindled into a mere listener or viewer—more than could be learned in the same
time with a little effort, or that the mechanical method has
any virtue other than the fact that such effort is not required?
Is there anything a picture can teach the pupil which is
worth as much as that ability to read which he stands in
very great danger of losing?

What those who so earnestly discuss the problems of communication seem to forget is that its success depends upon
the sensitivity of the listener as well as upon the efficiency of
the transmitter. Or as Shakespeare knew, the prosperity of a
jest lies in the ear of him that hears it. What is the use of
trying to make the jests simpler and simpler if the ears for
which they are destined are to grow duller and duller? It is

not a little learning but a little capacity for learning which is a dangerous thing.

Yet it is just the ability (or the willingness) to learn which no one seems to think should be insisted upon or even encouraged. Instead we "develop our techniques of communication" to the limit, even if that means (as it did in the army and does to some extent in the schools) teaching patriotism through comic books, mathematics by moving pictures, and the principles of ethics as they can be expounded in jingles very much like those used to urge upon us a particular cereal or hair tonic. Though most educated people seem to be agreed that the "commercial" is one of the ugliest and most humiliating phenomena of our civilization, some of these same people do not seem to realize how close they come to wanting to make "popular education" one long commercial designed to sell science, culture, and right political thinking to a public less and less willing really to think at all about anything.

In defense of this willingness to compete with the entertainer and the advertiser on his own level, the old argument against letting the devil have all the good tunes is often invoked. Why should selfish interests be permitted to remain so far ahead of everybody else in the technique of effective communication? We are told that the educator must wake up and catch up. He must take the instruments away from his opponents. They sell toothpaste and soap. They boast of creating "psychological wants" which nobody had until he was taught to have them. It is up to us to sell tolerance, good will, the scientific attitude, and even, perhaps, wisdom itself by similarly proved methods.

That there is a catch in all this, nobody seems to be very

much aware. But there is a catch, and the catch is this: The methods of the advertiser and the propagandist are not really usable for any purposes other than their own. They want their audiences to be as passive and uncritical as possible. Their methods are calculated not merely to make that audience believe what it is told, but also to believe just because it has been told. Their aim is to hypnotize and condition. The last thing they want is any thinking-for-yourself. Like the Bellman who went hunting for the snark, they have almost convinced even themselves that "what I tell you three times is true." Hence, what they are engaged in is not a kind of education but the direct opposite of education. The end result of their skill in one kind of communication is a group of listeners and "viewers" who are less than ignorant; it is a group which knows things that are not true and has become increasingly incapable of learning anything.

Nothing more clearly distinguishes a method of education from a technique of indoctrination than the fact that education demands from the subject some effort, especially some effort of attention, while propaganda does not. The advertiser will go to any length to make everything easy. The educator will see to it that something is expected of his pupil. He knows that no one can learn anything worth knowing unless he is willing to learn, as well as willing to be taught. He knows that learning how to learn is more important than any specific thing he can "communicate." And the grand question has now become whether or not the new techniques of mass communication inevitably and by their very nature weaken the power to learn at the same time that they make being taught so easy.

What so many enthusiasts of communication will not realize is that there is a point beyond which everything should not be made varied, vivid, picturesque, dramatic, and "interesting." A time is sure to come when something which needs very much to be learned cannot possibly be made as vivid, picturesque, dramatic, and interesting as certain other things. And when that time comes, only the individual who can turn his attention to what is most important, rather than allow it to be captured by what is most interesting, is capable of being educated. A population entrusted with the power to make decisions but incapable of sustained attention is in a parlous condition.

·VIII·

The Nemesis of Power

Platitudes, like folk songs, are usually anonymous. Even when they come into fashion during some remembered hour of history, the credit or the blame can seldom be assigned to an individual man. But, as everybody knows, it was Lord Acton who said, "All power tends to corrupt; absolute power corrupts absolutely." And that has become, among intellectuals, one of the most familiar of platitudes.

We accept it as true of both individuals and governments. No man and no organization can, we believe, be trusted with unlimited or even with very great power. He or it may be virtuous to begin with but will do ill in the end. Power is both evil and the cause of evil. Men cannot be like gods because they will become devils instead.

Strangely enough, however, what we assert of individuals, of governments, of groups, and even of nations, we do not believe of mankind itself. We look with suspicion on the individual who has risen too high; we devise checks and balances designed to limit economic groups and political parties; very recently we have begun to urge nations to limit their sovereignty voluntarily. But we still rejoice in every addition to the power which mankind as a whole can exercise and never assume that it also might become a victim of *hubris*.

We take, to begin with, enormous satisfaction in the seemingly endless advance of technology. Though the speed at which we can move, the rate at which we can manufacture goods, and the extent to which we can alter the face of the earth, have increased more during the last half-century than from the beginning of history up to that time, we take it for granted that this is good at least in itself. We take pride of the same kind in the successive discovery of one fundamental *source* of power after another because we know that each will make still further technological advances possible. We may be somewhat alarmed at the destructive possibilities of the very newest of all, but we call attention to its possible "peaceful uses" and assume that it, also, is at least potentially good.

In still more general terms we congratulate ourselves also upon the fact that we are learning not only to "control" nature but to control human nature as well. To the economist and the sociologist that means that he can "plan" societies and "condition" populations. To the biologist it means something even more inclusive. It means, so he says, that we are coming now to intervene in evolution itself. We did not create ourselves, did not choose to be what we now are. But we will have more and more to say about what we are going to become.

The Nemesis of Power

We recognize, of course, that power can be, and sometimes has been, misused. We discuss, sometimes, the methods by which it might be brought under better control. But it does not occur to us to consider that human societies, like the individual men of whom they are composed, might be the worse rather than the better for power too nearly unlimited. We do not admit the possibility that of societies as a whole it may also be true that "All power tends to corrupt; absolute power corrupts absolutely."

Perhaps we are wiser, less selfish, and more far-seeing than we were even two hundred years ago. But we are still imperfectly all these good things, and since the turn of the century it has been remarked more and more frequently that neither wisdom nor virtue have increased as rapidly as the need for both. Foolish or evil intentions can be more efficiently implemented than ever before. We may not be as eager to destroy our fellow men as we were then, but when we do yield to the impulse we can kill and lay waste far more effectively than ever before. And what is true of deliberate destruction is no less true of merely reckless self-indulgence.

We understand better that the earth is exhaustible, that man defaces as well as adorns the planet upon which he lives, that the concentration of populations and the interdependence of communities expose us to catastrophes incomparably more terrible than the merely local misfortunes which fell upon isolated communities. But greater knowledge does not bring proportionately greater wisdom. Worst of all, perhaps, we are far more competent than our forefathers ever were to misinform, mislead, and play upon the passions of men. Though all, so we like to think, are now within reach of the information and exhortation which goes out over the air, the fact remains that all are equally exposed to the lies and corruption which, as a matter of fact, actually monopolize the ears of something not too far from half the population of the globe. At this very moment, more lies than truths are being told over the air waves.

We may like to believe that we would not now make many of the mistakes made in the past, but during that past mankind was saved as much by its helplessness as by its power or its wisdom. The earth was too big to be more than lightly scarred, human nature too resilient to be more than partially corrupted, nature too powerful to be more than slightly modified by man's feeble attempts to have his way with her. Even to this day that "conquest of nature" of which we boast is an ideal rather than a fact. There are still more things outside our control than under it. But the number is decreasing. The balance swings in our direction. "Conquest" is an ominous word. In the moment of triumph we may discover that what we have conquered is ourselves.

The discovery that atomic power can be released may not in itself influence the outward aspect of men's lives as much as it was influenced by steam or electricity. As a matter of fact, Harrison Brown, a highly competent authority, has expressed the opinion that the actual amount of energy made available is less than that now being tapped in coal and oil. But because we have had more experience than the contemporaries of Watt and of Faraday had with the consequences of the discovery of a new source of power, and more especially because of the dramatic suddenness with which the possibilities of atomic energy were revealed, this is the first time that a majority of intelligent men have had forced upon their attention the fact that, in a specific instance, we may have more to fear than to hope from a sudden acquisition of power.

For the first time it has been clearly realized that the "control" upon which we were accustomed to congratulate ourselves is not general but limited. We can make an individual bomb explode when and where we will, but, just as steam and electricity were in a sense uncontrollable once they were turned loose upon the world and, for good or ill, determined what the society we lived in would be like, so too the ultimate consequences of the release of atomic energy are unpredictable.

Man has called many spirits from the vasty deep, released many genii from many bottles. They seem eager to do his bidding, but at most they obey only his specific commands. What the larger effects of these specific commands will be he never knows. And what is perhaps still more ominous, there is a command which the genii will never obey: "Get you back into your bottle!"

It is commonly said that what we need is more good will, or, in plainer terms, less inclination to take the killing of one another as so much a matter of course. And so we do. The world really is increasingly, if still inadequately, aware of the dangers of total war. But what it seems less inclined to consider is the less spectacular penalties it pays for increasing power to do both good and ill to itself. We eagerly exercise new powers, hope too easily for the best, and then struggle with the consequences as they come along—as we did with those of the industrial revolution.

Up to the present, mankind may have profited more than it has suffered from the various powers it has been able to exercise. Let us assume that it has. But that is, at best, no more than good luck. At no moment has it ever known or, indeed, seriously considered what the consequences were likely to be. What actually happens when the steam engine or the dynamo or, for that matter, the automobile, the airplane, and the radio, is invented is simply this: Our hearts lift up and we let out a glad cry, "Hold on to your hats boys, here we go again."

Even if it is assumed that more good than evil has always resulted so far, the results have certainly not all been unqualifiedly good. There was a time when the whole question of the industrial revolution hung in the balance. For a generation it enslaved children and they were freed just in the nick of time—i.e., just before child slavery could become an accepted social institution. At the present moment millions of children instead of standing in front of looms are seated in a seemingly milder enslavement before "giant twenty-one-inch screens," hypnotized by distant and usually anonymous masters who find it profitable in one way or another when certain images, sounds, and reiterated statements are presented to the eyes and ears of their victims.

It was nothing like this which Marconi, De Forest and the rest intended. Neither was it the enslavement of children nor the creation of poisonous smog clouds that Watt intended. But all these things were among the direct consequences. Who knows how this generation of children is to be set free?

Do we think that, so far, the price paid for power has never been too high? Perhaps we do. And perhaps we are right. But as the genii we release from bottles become more and more powerful, the assurance that we may bring them ultimately under some kind of control grows less and less. That this is true of weapons, many are beginning to fear. But may the danger from the other quarter be even greater because it is less recognized and harder to anticipate? Is it just possible that civilization will save itself from atomic weapons only to be destroyed by "the peaceful uses of atomic energy"? In the past, Western civilization has reeled under lesser impacts. Our globe has been scarred, plundered, and weighted down. Soils have been exhausted, animals exterminated, and rivers diverted. And if until yesterday the earth smiled at man's small efforts to change her face or upset her balance, the bulldozer now alters her more in a week than was once possible in a year. Then nature was stronger than we, but the time may come when she will be able to reassert herself only by reducing us to impotence again.

Within a generation, our way of life was revolutionized so completely that we can hardly imagine how existence was possible before the automobile and the telephone. What is more ominous is the fact that, by now, we actually could not do without them. Technology made large populations possible; large populations now make technology indispensable. A really drastic breakdown anywhere in the chain of mutually dependent machines would soon bring the whole complex to a halt. And by comparison with the consequences of cities deprived of power and unable either to bring in the goods they consume to get rid of rubbish they discard, the Black Death would be merely an unfortunate incident. Our very power, or rather our dependence upon it, has made us dreadfully vulnerable.

Some paragraphs back—if not, indeed, after the first two —even the more patient readers will probably have lost their patience. They will say as Voltaire said to Rousseau, "You almost persuade me to go on all fours." And they will add: "If, as you seem to hint, the automobile was a mistake, why then so, no doubt, was the wheeled cart, since the wheel, as every anthropologist knows, was one of the boldest and most fateful of man's inventions. If we actually did abandon the bulldozer for the digging stick and the power saw for the ax then some viewer-with-alarm would recommend that we use our teeth like beavers and abandon agriculture entirely in favor of nut gathering and berry picking. Animals began assuming the risks of power as soon as they dared to have brains, and apes seem to have begun using tools long before any ape man undertook to make them. To life and to opportunity we must say 'yea' or 'nay' and I am not sorry that man is a yea-sayer."

As humbly as possible let me reply: first, that I did not affirm that the automobile was unfortunate; second, that to say "Too much power corrupts" is not to say that powerlessness is desirable; and third, that I do not presume to know when in the past, or at what point in the future, man came or will come to the point where he is too powerful for his own good. Neither did I say that he could, or should, "simplify"!

As a matter of fact he certainly could not—except possibly by an extremely slow process—simplify at all without catastrophe. In all probability he will have to go along, if he can with the complexities of modern life. But the realization of this necessity is the strongest of reasons why it might be well —if indeed it should turn out to be possible—to think twice before we make any effort to make the modern world ever more complex. Thoreau might say of all the machinery of power what he did say of mere material possessions: "Unfortunately these things are more easily acquired than go id of." As so many have realized, we are saddled already with atomic weapons, the most terrible of all the "things" that are in the saddle and ride mankind.

We like to assure ourselves that nature, once we have learned her laws, will do our bidding. Actually we are like the sorcerer's apprentice, who could start the water flowing out could not make it stop. Or, to put it another way, we have used up the three wishes our fairy godmother granted us and we cannot avoid the consequences of the last one. The genii will not get back into their bottles and now we couldn't get along without them if they would.

Consider the case of the automobile, for whose convenience we pay a very high price. Bergan Evans cites from *Science News Letter* the statement that it has killed more than a million in the United States alone during the past forty years and that this is nearly twice as many as were killed in all the wars we have engaged in. Many organizations are now devoted to the prevention of war and they profess to be appalled by its destruction of life. But if that is what really concerns them, then why should they not immediately transform themselves into societies for the prevention of the automobile instead? How many advances in medicine has the horseless carriage canceled?

Comparatively speaking, the American record is not, as one might have guessed, a bad one. According to *Time*, France has over four times as many fatal traffic accidents per hundred thousand drivers as we have, and during the course of his career one French driver out of every eleven kills at least one person. But we seem determined to catch up if possible. Though statistics reveal (I am still relying on

Evans) that the better the roads the higher the acciden
rate, the cost of supplying our current "needs" for bette
and more dangerous highways was estimated in 1950 a
sixty billion dollars.

Perhaps this price in lives and money is worth paying fo
our increased mobility. Most people obviously think that i
is. Few would want to give up their Sunday excursion o
the ability to travel when and where they like. I certainly an
among those who wouldn't. But our civilization as a whol
does not really have any choice.

Suppose the price we pay got higher and higher until i
reached a point where it no longer seemed worth paying
Suppose, for example, the suspicion that gasoline fumes are ;
major cause of lung cancer should be confirmed and suppose
that the incidence of cancer should rise so tremendousl
that we could no longer shrug it off. What could we do? Re
strict the use of automobiles to the essential services and for
bid their use except for that transportation of the goods with
out which whole populations would starve?

That would be not only difficult to do but catastrophic i
done. Our economic system is dependent upon the industry
which manufactures these instruments of pleasure, necessity
and death. If that industry were seriously curtailed, so mucl
unemployment would be created and so much of that "pur
chasing power" upon which we depend would disappear
that other industries would grind almost to a halt and w
should be faced with a depression by comparison with whicl
that following the crash of 1929 would seem like boom time

Once we lived without the automobile and without ;
thousand other things. But we could not live without them
now. One by one we acquired them only to become depend

ent upon them. We think we own them, but they own us. Economists and sociologists take it more and more for granted that industry rules us. What we do, how we live, and even what we think we want, all depend upon industry's needs rather than upon ours.

Obviously, then, there is not much use talking about a return to the horse-and-buggy age. Conceivably, civilization might take a slow turn and gradually simplify itself. Much more probably, it might be so drastically simplified by some overwhelming catastrophe like an all-out world war that the few survivors might, willy-nilly, resume a pastoral or even a hunting economy capable of supporting the very small remaining population. But technological advance is a process which is not likely to prove reversible as the result of any deliberate intention on our part. None of the power we have acquired will be voluntarily surrendered in the near future. Even nations and races far less enthusiastic than we about "progress" find themselves carried along in the current. France is dragged protesting into twentieth-century civilization. Even the Navajos, one of the most conservative of all peoples, have turned into hunters of uranium.

Moreover, it does not appear that we have any disposition even to look before we make still another leap, to examine the probable consequences of the wishes we are wishing or to ask what genii are in the bottles with whose corks we are already toying. To the private automobile, the private jet plane is about to be added.

A great rocket expert has recently expressed the opinion that "push-button" travel over great distances is in immediate prospect. Science fiction delights its devotees with the promise of interplanetary wars, and children in space helmets slaughter their playmates with "disintegrators." Always it is the same dream, or nightmare, that is being pursued. If our grandfathers could hardly have been persuaded to believe that we would accept with no more than a shrug highways strewn with bleeding corpses, is there any reason to suppose that our children will be much disturbed by a tenfold increase in traffic accidents or that they will be any less inclined than we to take "Well we get there faster, don't we?" as an adequate answer to any criticism. Tennyson imagined the day when

. . . there rain'd a ghastly dew
From the nation's airy navies grappling in the central blue.

That day is come. How long will it be before there is added to that ghastly dew the blood, limbs, and entrails of happy picnic parties off for a Sunday at their favorite luncheon spot halfway around the globe?

Is that what we want? Is it a necessary part of the richer fuller life for everybody we are always promising ourselve when we have "progressed" just a little further? If it is no what we want, then what weakness in ourselves makes us accept it?

Is it, possibly, that we ourselves do not know what leads u on? We believe that we are interested in power only because power can serve humanity, but sometimes we seem to have forgot our professed aims; we seem to be interested in power as an end rather than a means; to admire *virtù* or effective ness for its own sake so that it is the supposed glory rathe than the utility of power which has come to fascinate us Does that not suggest both the way in which power corrupt and a criterion by which we may judge whether or not we are being corrupted? It may be impossible to say at just what point we became too powerful, but it is possible to say that the point has been passed when we begin to consider power itself the most obvious good we can pursue.

The typical science-fiction story is today's dream of tomorrow but the dream has changed since H. G. Wells popularized it. The world which it now imagines is no longer better, or even more convenient, more comfortable, and more abundant. It is, instead, a world increasingly precarious and full of larger violences. The One World (or One Solar System, or One Universe) which has there been established is not a oneness in which planets live at peace with each other but one in which they are closer only in the sense that enmity can now reach out across space and malevolence across the barrier which distance formerly established. Yet this future is usually presented as a promise rather than a threat. Why? Is it not exclusively because these men of the future are more powerful than we?

Since the beginning of the scientific age, there have been differing conceptions of what science was "for." Quite properly it was sometimes regarded as "useful" and sometimes as valuable simply because it increased understanding. But though pure science is a legitimate pursuit, pure technology (i.e., technology regarded as an end in itself) is antihuman —and it is to that we have come. The machine rather than man has become the measure of all things and we regard the improvement, even the welfare, of man's tools as more important than man's own.

We are no longer much surprised when we hear, for example, that a rocket expert who designed weapons for one of our enemies shrugs his shoulders when asked to work for us instead. He is not interested, we say, in politics. But that is not quite adequate. Actually, he is simply not interested in what rockets are to be used for. He is interested simply in rockets—which is to say in machines (or power) for its own sake. And though this attitude is only occasionally so dramatically revealed, millions have unconsciously adopted it. If we worshiped only the machines which *make* things, we might say that we were materialists. But we are almost equally impressed by those which merely *do* things— which go faster, or higher, or further. We do not, like a utilitarian, ask what good they are or, like a materialist, what we can get out of them. Like the members of many primitive religious cults, we are uncertain whether the powers we worship are evil or good; we are sure only that they are powerful and that, therefore, they should be worshiped.

Since man first recognized or suspected power outside himself, he has worshiped many strange gods, adored them in many strange rituals and sacrificed himself to them in many strange ways. He has slaughtered animals and maidens; he has whipped, starved, and mutilated himself. He has slept on nails, gazed at the sun until blind, and held his arms aloft until they withered. It was not himself but the god of his idolatry whom he was determined to serve. And so it is again with us. To Thoreau, the inhabitants of his own Concord "appeared to be doing penance in a thousand remarkable ways." What would he think of the new ways devised since his time?

If the Marxists are right and man neither is nor can be anything except what his independently evolving technology makes him; if not only his way of life but his standards, his desires, and his understanding of the universe are simply by-products of that logic of *things* which he cannot alter, then there is no use trying to do anything other than what we actually are doing—namely, either await with resignation or anticipate with joy the fulfillment already implicit at this beginning of the Age of Power. We must merely, as the saying is, co-operate with the inevitable.

But if the Marxists are wrong and the "control of nature" need not be pure illusion, if we are not made by our environment but may make it instead, then it is worthwhile to ask what new direction we might be able to take when we become convinced (if we are not convinced already) that we are paying too high a price for the power acquired and that it is obviously no longer a paradox to call machines the masters rather than the servants of mankind?

It is difficult to imagine that we could be persuaded to give up what we have now. It is still more difficult to imagine how we could do so even if we wanted to. Only a few individuals can live by Walden Pond and only a few more in Brook Farms or in what, I believe, are now called "intentional communities." Yet it is only somewhat less obvious that the mere determination to make better use in the future than we have in the past of the power which increases at an increasing rate is not sufficient. We have, in two centuries, made little progress in that direction. We have, indeed, made so little that it seems more likely now than it has at any time since the age of technology began that we may be literally destroyed by the power we have acquired. The machine is still winning and will continue to win as long as we continue to take the attitude we do take; as long as even those not wholeheartedly committed to the worship of power for its own sake are nevertheless content to welcome its increases first and to think what to do about them later.

·IX·

The Meaning of the Meaningless Question

Those who celebrate without qualification the success of our civilization in solving the problems it has most wanted to solve often add something else: that success began a few centuries ago when we learned for the first time what questions to ask. Very tardily, so they say, we stopped wasting our time on problems to which there is no solution. We ceased trying to know the unknowable, to measure the unmeasurable, and to touch the intangible.

No indisputable progress, they point out, had ever been made in metaphysics, moral philosophy, or theology. There was—and there still is—no more general agreement about the distinguishing characteristics of the good or the beautiful than there was in Plato's time. But just so soon as we came to accept the fact that the field of our competence is technology rather than what used to be called wisdom we began, so they say, to outdistance all our predecessors in *making* and *doing*.

By now we have discovered so many facts about the physical world that no expert can possibly know more than a very small proportion of them. We have learned how to do so many different and astonishing things that only by a carefully planned program of training in the various skills can we hope to keep functioning a society utterly dependent upon them. Nor are all the things we have learned to do confined to technology in the most limited sense. We not only produce abundance but also distribute it—at least more equitably than it was ever distributed before. We are even, so we believe, learning rapidly how to control what men will think, want, and believe as well as how they will live. And all this has come about because so large a proportion of the available intelligence has been usefully applied to the investigation of solvable problems.

Most of what is desirable in the present condition of man is the result of this success in answering the questions he has been so intent upon asking. Nor are all the desirable results material. Hardly less obvious than the creation of abundance, comfort, and that very dubious "security" which he has come to enjoy are certain changes in our intellectual attitudes brought about by a vastly increased understanding of the mechanical aspects of the universe in which we live.

Once almost everything about that physical universe was mysterious, unpredictable, and without any understood relation to anything else. The uncontrollable, the unexpected, and the seemingly arbitrary was everywhere; the dependable, related, and manageable a rare exception. The physical universe was one in which, so far as men knew, almost anything might be true and almost anything might happen. By the end of the nineteenth century it had come to seem, on the other hand, that ours was a universe in which only a very limited number of things could happen and in which, so we thought, we already knew what most of them were.

In moments of criticism and caution scientists themselves sometimes pointed out that their answers were always answers to the question "how" rather than "why" and also, what is equally important, that they were (as Karl Pearson put it) no more than descriptions of "what happens," not at all what could be called in any full sense an "explanation" of the universe. But many converts to the scientific method as a philosophy have tended to confuse the "description of what happens" with an understanding of the thing itself. When we ask successfully of any object or any phenomena what its origins are, what developments it has undergone, what predictable regularities can be observed, and with what other phenomena it is analogous we often feel that it has been "explained"—though in actual fact we have merely explained it away. This habit of mind sharpens one kind of awareness but tends to dull another because all such "explanations" are, in one sense, deceptive. What they come down to is no more than a more detailed description which distracts attention from what remains fundamentally inexplicable in the thing itself.

One may take as a simple example the lithographed chart exhibited in many classrooms. It is labeled "How We Hear," and it pictures in half-diagrammatic form the external ear, the drum, the anvil, and the semicircular canal. But this is not at all "how we hear." It is only how vibrations in the air are transmitted. Hearing begins where the diagram stops. Hearing is the experience or the conscious awareness of sound. And conscious awareness is not in any way or to any extent "explained" by anything which can be represented in a mechanical diagram. The ear and the eye no more explain hearing and sight than a telescope explains the logical de-ductions made by an astronomer who looks through it or, for that matter, his sense of awe when he contemplates one of the nebulae. Anyone who is taught by the chart to believe that he now knows "how we hear" has lost more than he has gained. In a sense he is more ignorant than he was when he thought he did not know.

Another simple illustration might be drawn from a recent and generally admirable semipopular textbook on plant physiology, one chapter of which is headed "Science Explains Heredity." This chapter first gives a clear account of what is known about the Mendelian law, though it may be said to "explain" heredity only in one very limited sense. There then follows an equally good account of what has been learned since Mendel's time about the chromosomes and the genes which, in a similar sense, may be said to "explain" Mendelian laws. Both Mendel's explanation and the explanation of the explanation are, in one meaning, perfectly valid. They are, that is to say, perfectly valid if by explana-tion is meant simply a fuller account of the stages of a proc-ess and of the devices which it involves.

But "explanation" is a tricky word. We tend to assume that when a thing has been thus in one sense explained it has also been "explained" in a different sense. The fact re-mains that after "science explains heredity," heredity is in another sense as mysterious and as wonderful as it was be-fore. You might fully explain a watch to one who had never seen one by taking it out of its case and showing how the wheels go 'round. But you have not to the same extent explained heredity when you reveal its wheels going 'round, and it is one of the great delusions of our time that you have. The fundamental error is the error which consists in failing to realize that explanation in terms of the "how" can never be more than explanation in a very limited sense.

Wordsworth despised that kind of inquirer who would "peep and botanise upon his mother's grave." Keats expressed the same attitude more explicitly when he exclaimed in dismay that at the cold touch of philosophy "all charms fly." But both were wrong in so far as they assumed that the one kind of knowledge actually does remove mystery and the occasion for wonder. They were right only in so far as they foresaw that many who devoted themselves to the acquisition of this kind of knowledge would come to believe that they "understood" what they did not understand at all.

The search for the one kind of knowledge and for no other kind is the legitimate enterprise of science when science is properly defined as the accumulation of this kind of knowledge about everything concerning which this kind of knowledge is possible. But Science itself is misleading and stultifying when it denies or forgets that other kinds of knowledge involving direct awareness of the thing itself rather than of "the way it works" is possible. Modern man has far more knowledge of the one kind than his forefathers had, but he has less of the other. Some sacrifice of it has necessarily been involved in the pursuit of the scientific kind, but however desirable it may once have been to make the sacrifice in exchange for the practical benefits which have resulted from the prodigious increase in knowledge of "the way things work," the time has come to call attention to the sacrifice itself and to recover, if possible, some of that lost knowledge which is impossible without a more direct awareness than we usually now have of "things in themselves."

As we have learned more and more "about" the universe and "about" our own consciousness we have become less and less aware of much that is worth recognizing in both the universe without and the universe within. Biology has taught us almost everything we know "about" the phenomenon which we call "being alive"; psychology has taught us what we know "about" consciousness and patterns of behavior. But they have tended to make us less aware of life and of consciousness themselves than we might or should be. We know all "about" love—about the functioning of the sex glands, about the libido, and about sublimation. We describe, account for, and "explain" it all. But we know less, not only of love, but even of the emotions connected with the gratification of the sex instinct than those who could experience either with a greater intensity just because they knew less "about" them and were less convinced that they could explain them away. Perhaps "knowledge about" does not necessarily diminish "knowledge of," but we have permitted it to do so.

This is the reason we have so immeasurably surpassed all previous ages in invention and in what we call "the control of nature," but it is also the reason why so many previous ages have immeasurably surpassed us in the arts. The poet (in the broadest meaning of the term) is the man whose attention is fixed upon the thing itself, who is aware of it, who has experience with it, and who is therefore concerned with "knowledge of," not with "knowledge about." This is indeed the source of the delight which poets give us and which so often consists in the sudden, surprised awareness of the thing itself together with the realization that we have hardly noticed it in our determination to trace its origin, discover its processes, and formulate its "laws."

In certain untypical contemporary writers and artists (Aldous Huxley, for instance) a sense of the incompleteness of "explanation" and "knowledge about" has become so acute that they have returned to a mysticism which rejects completely all reliance upon the kinds of knowing which most moderns have tended to accept as the only genuine ones. They rely entirely upon intuition and "vision," by means of which, so they assert, they are put into direct contact with ultimate reality in all its strangeness and beauty. There are few human beings who have not experienced brief moments of intense awareness not wholly different from those which the mystics describe—sometimes provided by some such simple process as staring at themselves in the mirror or indulging the childish trick of repeating one word over and over again while trying to concentrate upon its meaning. At such moments there is a sudden realization that despite all one knows about man in general, about the laws of psychology and all the rest of it, one does not actually know even oneself at all.

From such experiences the experience of the mystic differs only in its clarity and intensity. Both involve a direct awareness of the thing itself. They are truly a kind of knowledge, knowledge *of*, not knowledge *about*. It is not, to be sure, "useful knowledge" but may be something better. The one is only a means to an end. The other is an end in itself. And the capacity for it may well be the most completely unique of the privileges which man alone enjoys. It may distinguish him more clearly from the other animals than the reason which he sometimes comes close to or than the tool-using of which some animals are clearly capable. Perhaps only man can know a thing or love a thing for itself alone.

It may be readily granted that if a society which recognizes no knowledge except "knowledge about" is in danger of becoming something less than human, one which entirely neglects that kind of knowledge is doomed—so at least history seems to suggest—to suffer in poverty, squalor, and disease the penalty of knowing too little about how the physical universe works. But it is not evident that there is any necessity of choosing the one or the other exclusively, and it may very well be that the present condition of man would be a better one if he had more awareness of what the mystics, both ancient and contemporary, have to say.

Even less disputably would it seem to be true that we would be wise not to dismiss so completely as we now usually do all the questions to which positive answers cannot be given but which remain tremendously important nevertheless. Are they, as so many would say, "meaningless" questions, or are they merely very difficult? Are we, on the whole, better for refusing to ask whatever we cannot definitively answer? Or is there something to be gained—something which once was gained and now is lost—by the mere conscious posing of such questions? Have we really got rid of the problems implied by dismissing them?

Do not all people—even the most explicit relativists—actually give pragmatic answers to such questions as "What constitutes a good life?" though they usually give them without ever having considered the basis of their judgment? Has not our society actually given thoughtless and nearly random answers to all those questions which are, so it likes to assure itself, "meaningless"? If they are, in fact, meaningful rather than meaningless, then they must be raised before it is possible to ask whether the actual condition of man is what it ought to be or whether it is moving in that direction. And that is a question we do not ask.

The material aspects of our condition lend themselves to precisely the kind of investigation we have learned so well how to make. Never before was our condition investigated in so many of these aspects or by such efficient techniques. Man's effectiveness as a producer and his preferences as a consumer have been measured, analyzed, and statistically presented. The hours which he devotes to labor, the wages he receives, and the prices he pays for the goods he buys have been studied and the figures for one nation, or class, or region have been compared with the others. We know how long he lives and from what diseases he suffers. We know how much schooling he gets, how many children he has, how many bathrooms he can afford. We know also what sports he is interested in, what churches he belongs to, what political ideas he holds. And upon many of these things we conduct frequent checks so that we know also both the minor fluctuations in his income and the waverings of his loyalty to movie stars, television comedians, and crooners.

So far as such aspects of his condition are concerned we have documented them with an amazing and sometimes absurd thoroughness. In previous ages men have usually had only a vague idea of what their material condition was. Today they know. And yet the literature, the philosophy, and the art of some previous ages give the impression that they knew very much better what, in other respects, their condition was than we know what, in those respects, ours is.

If this is true, is it not because they had incorporated into their consciousness some of that kind of awareness which is the mystic's exclusive concern, or, to put it another way, because they neither confused "a description of what happens" with "an explanation" nor dismissed as "meaningless" (and therefore answered without examining them) all those fundamental questions to which the positivist can give no answer.

Perhaps the paradox of a wealthy and powerful civilization which is nevertheless insecure, anxious, and alienated cannot be resolved until we too come to realize that the answers given consciously or unconsciously to "meaningless questions" are, in actual fact, what determine the character of a civilization.

What, then, are some of the questions which could be asked but nowadays so seldom are? Or what, more boldly, is the most important question a man *can* ask? Is it only, as some would say, "What kind of society provides for the most equitable system of production and distribution?" Or is it, to go to the opposite extreme, "Does God exist?"

These questions are the archetypes of a whole set of variations every one of which involves the same issue. If, for instance, you ask whether or not there are any moral absolutes which man disregards at his peril you are asking at least part of what the question "Does God exist?" implies. If you ask instead, "What sort of education should the citizen be given to assure him a proper adjustment to the world in which he lives?" you are choosing a member of the family to which the first question belongs. And your choice implies a choice of premises. Either this is a universe which man did not make and which therefore he cannot fundamentally change, or the universe in which he lives is, both physically and morally, whatever he makes it.

Most men today would prefer not to bring God into it. For one thing the word has been defined in too many ways to be surely meaningful. Besides, even a precise definition would commit us to dealing with something too large and too remote for a rational answer in terms of our experience. But one can very easily ask a question which is a member of the family to which "Does God exist?" belongs.

"Does human nature exist?" Are there, that is to say, beliefs, enterprises, and ways of life which are not, and never can be, consonant with that nature? Or can human nature adapt and adjust to anything? Should we, for example, ask not merely what kind of society would provide for the most efficient and equitable system of production and distribution but also what kind would be most in accord with human nature? Should we ask not merely what education best fits a man for living in his world, but also what kind of world would best accord with his nature?

Such questions have been increasingly unpopular since Hobbes gave one answer by expounding the theory of what Locke was to call the *tabula rasa*. But much—one might say everything—with which this present discussion is concerned depends upon the answer one assumes or gives. Take *tabula rasa* as a complete description of the brain with which a man is born and all the relativisms, moral, social, cultural, and aesthetic, logically follow. On a blank slate anything can be written. If what is commonly called human nature is merely whatever the existing condition of man makes it, then there is no basis for any criticism of that condition and those who believe that the business of education is to teach the student "adjustment to the existing culture" are on unassailable ground. "The normal" has no meaning other than "the average" and men ought to do whatever it is that they do do. Vice is not a creature of hideous mien unless you have been brought up to call something "vice" and to call it hideous.

In a hundred different ways the critical minority has told us that our society has no "unity," no "traditions," no "standards"; that there is nothing we live "by" or "for." As one clinical psychologist, saying again what has so often been said, recently put it: "The trouble with our age for both parents and children is that we no longer have *any* strong convictions as to what is 'reasonable' for society." But we have not "lost" that unity, those traditions and standards, or those strong convictions "as to what is 'reasonable' for society." They have been taken away from us by the different group of intellectuals who have convinced us that such standards, traditions, and convictions are actually merely prejudices of a particular culture and unworthy of an intelligent man capable of reason or of learning the lesson which anthropology teaches. Thus while one group bewails our loss the other professes to set us free.

What we are said to have lost can hardly be restored by those who have, at a minimum, helped us lose it. Neither the sociologists who maintain that in our particular society "normal" means merely "average" nor the anthropologists who add that this is always true in any society are likely to provide those whom they convince with traditions, standards, or a conviction concerning what is "reasonable" in society. If a norm is anything more than the average of what is, then it must have some sanctions somewhere. And ultimately that sanction must be found in either a law of God or a law of nature.

Either something outside man establishes them for him or he himself, by his own nature, establishes them for himself. Any society which, like our own, believes in no transcendent God but is beginning to be nervously aware of the dangers of remaining permanently without "any strong convictions as to what is 'reasonable' for society" might well address itself seriously to three questions. (1) Are there reasons for believing that in some respects human nature is constant and that to that extent man is something not wholly what changing conditions make him? (2) If the answer to this question is "yes," then is it possible for the human being to recognize some of these constants as distinguished from those changeable aspects of his seeming nature which do depend entirely upon the culture in which he grows up and the economic system under which he lives? (3) If this question also is answered in the affirmative, then is it possible to say that certain aspects of his present condition are sufficiently repugnant to that nature to suggest that this is one of the reasons why unprecedented power and prosperity have not made him so content or so serene as might have been expected?

Let us then address ourselves to the first of these questions.

·X·

The Not So Blank Slate

No offhand saying is more familiar than "You can't change human nature." Nevertheless, we are today much more likely to proceed upon the assumption that you can; and the whole of the prevalent, Marxist-tinged social philosophy takes it for granted that "human nature," far from being a constant, is nothing but a determined and predictable reaction to "society."

Moreover, that old-fashioned minority which says and really means, "You can't change human nature," is generally dismissed as reactionary and cynical. What they are usually assumed to mean (and what they very often do mean) is merely that man is incurably self-centered, selfish, envious, grasping, combative, greedy, mischievous, and cruel.

The possibly encouraging aspects of the assumption that there is something permanent about human nature and that it is changeable only within limits, is curiously overlooked. If man is incurably this or that unamiable thing he may

169

also be, incurably, this or that admirable or even noble thing. When liberals consider what the Nazi and Communist totalitarians have made the condition of millions to be and when they assume that this condition will prove intolerable in the end, they sometimes say that "sooner or later human nature will rebel." But it won't and it can't unless human nature is, indeed, an independent reality, not merely a product.

Even in the United States the same unanswered question arises in a milder form, because all proponents of a completely "planned society" also go on the assumption that human nature can be made to become whatever the social, political, and economic organization are designed to make it. To say to them that "you can't change human nature" *may* mean, as it often does, that you cannot condition man to the abandonment of all desire for personal profit, personal possessions, "status," and all the other prizes given to excellence. But it may also mean, perhaps, that you cannot make him the pure conformist and pure materialist which many "planned societies" seem to want to make him.

Considered thus, "You can't change human nature" may be an expression of the last best hope for an age which has lost faith in man as, in any sense, the captain of his soul. And since it does seem to suggest such a hope, then surely there is good reason to re-examine the so generally neglected assumption that there is, after all, some such thing as human nature, or, to put it in another way, that what we are born with is not a completely blank slate.

One had best begin by remembering that just such a re-examination of the theory was made during the eighteenth century for exactly the same reason that we would like to make it, and also that those who, for a time, did confidently reassert the reality of human nature were worsted a few generations later by that new wave of destructive criticism of which so much of today's thinking is a part.

The nihilistic conclusions which inevitably follow from the Hobbesian premise had been drawn by Hobbes himself and eagerly embraced by the intellectuals of his time, who felt themselves emancipated from the traditions of a soberer generation much as those of the nineteen twenties felt themselves emancipated from Victorianism. But after hardly more than a generation of exuberant Hobbesism the early eighteenth century began to put up its own fight against the nihilism to which, like us, it could no longer oppose traditional religious assumptions.

Its answer to the question, "To what shall we turn for guidance now that we no longer have God's revealed word?" was the concepts of nature and of right reason.

If, so it argued, the good cannot be defined as "that which is in accord with God's will" it is at least "that which is in accord with nature." And it proposed a simple criterion by which it thought that nature might be distinguished from custom or mere fashion. Whatever tastes, customs, or convictions vary radically from time to time and from place to place were recognized as mere matters of fashion. Whatever all men tended to agree upon was accepted as "in accord with nature."

The *Iliad*, for example, exemplified the natural laws of aesthetics because all men who had ever known it found it admirable. Because a belief in God seemed to be a universal characteristic of all societies this belief must also be natural, though none of the theological creeds which are so wildly variable and inconsistent are. Thus nature (including human nature) was presumed to set up its own absolutes.

What men should do was not, to them, whatever men do do, but rather what men have always thought they *should* do. Education was not, as we now think it should be, an "adjustment" to the prevailing or fashionable mores but to a life "in accordance with that right reason which understands and accepts the laws of nature." The best literature or music was not, as we now tend to think, whatever is at the moment preferred by the greatest number of people but what, in the long run, nature is seen to be striving toward.

Unfortunately, perhaps, this fight against the nihilistic implications of the blank slate and the relativism which follows logically from it turned out to be only a delaying action. Presently, the concept of nature was criticized out of existence just as that of God had been. There simply is not, said its critics, *anything* in religion, or morals, or art upon which, in actual fact, all men, or even nearly all men, have agreed.

The support and factual amplification of this criticism became one of the chief tasks of anthropology and sociology during the nineteenth and twentieth centuries. Before the first of these centuries was over, William Lecky in his very influential *History of European Morals* could write that there is no act which cannot be shown to have been forbidden as a sin at one time and place and enjoined as a duty at some other. And so, after the heroic struggle of the eighteenth century Lecky brought us back once more to the conviction that morals are merely mores; that neither God nor any permanent human nature gives sanction to one system of ethics rather than another. We were, in other words, given back the blank slate upon which anything can be written, and, on the whole, the twentieth century has accepted it.

Professor Leo Strauss, a present-day defender of the now usually discredited concept of natural right, has recently pointed out that the collapse of the eighteenth-century argument based upon "general consent" does not logically invalidate the concept itself:

" 'Consent of all mankind,' " he writes, "is by no means a necessary condition of the existence of natural right. Some of the greatest natural right teachers have argued that, precisely if natural right is rational, its discovery presupposes the cultivation of reason, and therefore natural right will not be known universally: one ought not even expect any real knowledge of natural right among savages."

This defense is applicable, not only to the concept of natural right, but equally to all the other phases of the more general concept of the natural as some sort of reality. But it is not likely to be very effective with most contemporary relativists because it assumes that reason, as distinct from rationalization, is possible and because it rules out as irrelevant the opinions and practices of the savage, the uncultivated, and the stupid upon which the relativists lean so heavily in drawing their conclusions concerning what is "natural" and "normal"!

Nevertheless, the fact remains that in a world which has so definitely rejected all transcendental sanctions for either codes of behavior or standards of value, "nature" and "human nature" seem to be the only possible place to look for a norm which is not merely an average or a concept of an "ought" which is more than a description of usual conduct. The question whether or not there is such a thing as human nature therefore remains for us the grandest of all living questions and makes it necessary for us to ask whether the usual negative answer really is justifiable and permanent or whether we shall some day swing again in a different direction and discover evidence now neglected that human nature really is something in itself and does provide certain absolutes, valid at least in the human realm.

Have the anthropologists been so preoccupied with the collection of materials to demonstrate the enormous *differences* between cultures that they have overlooked some things which really are common to them all? Have the experimental psychologists been so busy conditioning both animals and men that they have paid little attention to the resistance to conditioning which both can put up?

One little straw blowing in the winds of psychological doctrine seems to point in that direction. Some skeptics have begun to wonder whether instinct on the one hand and the conditioned reflex on the other really can account for all the behavior of living organisms. A brain which carries written upon it even a system of instincts is far from being a blank slate. But that is by no means all. Certain other sufficiently obvious facts have recently been emphasized: (1) Birds know by instinct how to fly and do not have to be taught. (2) Seals do not know instinctively how to swim but are very easily taught by their mothers to do so. (3) You would have a very hard time indeed teaching most songbirds to swim.

There are, in other words, not just two classes of animal behavior (inborn and learned) but also a third—that which is not inborn though the ability to learn it easily is.

Some to whom these facts have come home have begun to wonder whether the same may not be true, not only of skills, but throughout the whole psychic realm of beliefs, tastes, and motives. The thesis of the moral relativists is—to take an extreme case—that since no one was born with the "innate idea" that dishonesty and treachery are evil, then the conviction that they are evil can be nothing but the result of social education. The opposite, so they say, could just as easily be taught. Value judgments are therefore merely the rationalized prejudices of a given culture.

May not, in actual fact, the contrary be true, namely, that certain ideas are more *easily learned* than others; that what the eighteenth century called natural law, natural taste, and the rest is real and consists in those beliefs and tastes which are most readily learned and also most productive of health and happiness?

Perhaps you can condition an individual or a society to think and behave "unnaturally" just as you might possibly teach a robin to swim. But men who have been conditioned to think or behave unnaturally are as unhappy and as inefficient as swimming robins. As the biochemist Roger J. Williams puts it, "There are blanks and blanks. The blank brain of the child is capable as time goes on of accepting, digesting (perceiving), and acting upon a multitude of impressions that the brain of a rat is quite incapable of handling."

Is this belaboring the obvious? At least it is not anything so obvious that the implications have not been for long disregarded by those who preferred to disregard them. Perhaps no ideas are innate; but if the capacity to entertain readily some ideas and not others is innate, then it all comes down to much the same thing. Professor Williams has led us back by a new route to the eighteenth century and to one of the most discredited exponents of its ideas. "Nature affords at least a glimm'ring light;/The lines, tho' touch'd but faintly, are drawn right."

What Pope thought of as a metaphor may be an accurate biological statement. On the not quite blank slate the lines are touched too faintly to constitute an automatic instinct. They are much like the latent image on a photographic plate—imperceptible until developed. But what development will reveal already exists. There is such a thing as human nature. What we are born with is not a blank slate but a film bearing already a latent image.

No doubt—as Pope went on to say elsewhere, as experimental psychologists prove in the laboratory, and as educators as well as dictators have all too often demonstrated—the lines may be "o'er laid," and the unnatural cease to seem a creature of hideous mien. But the conditioners have to work at it—hard. Men believe in, for instance, the reality of good and evil much more readily than they can be made to accept cultural relativism.

Such an assumption is at least one which no valid science forbids, and if we make it we are saved from the nihilism of present-day cultural and moral relativism as the eighteenth century was saved from the nihilism of Hobbes. In a sense, God—or at least a useful substitute for Him—exists. We have again some point of reference now lacking in every inquiry which sets out to determine what kind of society, or education, or culture would be best for us. One thing is no longer as good as another provided only it can be shown, or made, to exist. We need no longer talk only about what can be *done to* men or what we might be able to *make* them into. We can talk again about what, in themselves, they *are*.

That involves what is certainly no easy inquiry. One of the most terrifying of Pascal's *Pensées* seems to range him with the enemy: "They say that habit is second nature; perhaps nature is only first habit." To distinguish correctly between the one and the other is one of the most difficult tasks we could set ourselves. But perhaps it is also the most important.

More than two thousand years ago when Herodotus was inventing cultural anthropology he noted a fact which anthropologists still make much of. Inquiring about funeral customs, he discovered that those who burned their dead were shocked when told that some peoples buried theirs and that the latter were no less shocked to learn that other human beings were so impious as to consign human bodies to the flames. On the basis of this fact Herodotus was already almost prepared to conclude what the nineteenth century hailed as a great and novel discovery, namely that morals are, after all, only mores. When in Rome you should do as the Romans do—not merely because that is the courteous way to behave but because the customs of the Romans are, in that latitude, what is truly right, seemly, and proper.

Does this necessarily follow in any such unqualified and unlimited sense? True, history may give us no reason to suppose that burying one's dead is more in accord with human nature than burning or that burning is more in accord with it than burying. But there is, nevertheless, a fact which neither Herodotus nor most recent cultural and moral relativists seem to have noticed: There is a good deal of evidence to support the contention that an enduring characteristic of the nature of man does bid him dispose of human remains in *some* traditional and ritual fashion. Burial customs of one kind or another appear so early in human prehistory that their existence may be one of the criteria for distinguishing between men and mere half-men, and some sort of respect for his dead may have been part of the nature of man for as long as there has been man to have a nature.

All such imperatives (if there are any) as originate in human nature itself must be, like that which bids man pay respect to his dead, highly generalized rather than specific. But even such highly generalized imperatives can have important consequences. The pure relativist who denies the existence of *anything* permanent in human nature and who then finds himself shocked by, let us say, the "atrocities" committed against the dead by Nazi authorities is logically bound to tell himself that he is merely reacting according to a prejudice unworthy of one who has come to understand intellectually that custom is never more than custom and that there is no reason why, for instance, corpses should not always be made into useful soap—as they were in Germany during the second world war.

But such "mere prejudices" may not be prejudices at all. They may be rather a revulsion against a practice which violates something fundamental in human nature, namely, that something which does not require burial rather than cremation or cremation rather than burial but does require ritual respect for the dead. Similarly, other Nazi attitudes toward, say, the victims of genocide may not be merely part of the unfamilar mores of another race but one of the clear signs that Nazism consists of a whole complex of principles and practices repugnant not merely to "prevalent ideas of right and wrong" but to the nature of man himself. Perhaps, indeed, the fundamental horror of Nazism may be just that it follows further than we have yet followed the implications of the relativism we profess without yet having so consistently implemented them.

If it is true that human nature does require some ceremonial respect for the bodies of the dead as a testimony of respect and an expression of awe in the face of death, then that fact will suggest another generalization. It may be true that cultures exhibit such a bewildering variety of actions and attitudes as to give a superficial air of probability to the conclusion that *all* moral ideas and all ideas of what constitutes propriety are no more than what limitlessly variable custom has established. Yet men almost invariably believe that *some* beliefs and *some* customs are right. However diverse and irreconcilable specific moral judgments are and have been, moral judgment itself has been a constantly continuing activity of the human mind. What no society has ever been able to believe for long is precisely the doctrine which ours has embraced—namely, that morals are no more than mores.

A sense that right and wrong (however difficult to determine) are nevertheless both real and tremendously important seems to be part of fundamental human nature. In simple societies no sanction other than custom may be needed to justify what is done or what is not done, because custom itself is naïvely accepted as the final arbiter and is not regarded as "mere" custom. The more intellectually sophisticated a society becomes, the more complicated the questions involved are seen to be, the more subtly they are investigated, and the less clear the answers.

But the conviction that the difference between right and wrong is tremendously important persists and has hardly been got rid of even in those societies which profess the most unqualified relativism. To state the proposition in the most general possible terms, it comes down to this: An obvious characteristic of the nature of man is his inveterate habit of making value judgments. Perhaps he is the only animal who can give rational form to his preferences or is capable of calling them by such names as The Good and The Beautiful. But he cannot be better defined than by saying that he is the animal which *can do* and *does insist upon doing* just that.

Yet this is the fact which the cultural relativists most strangely overlook, both when they profess to be purely objective and when, as has often been the case, they draw lessons or "morals" of their own. They point out how irreconcilable different sets of customs and different sets of values can be. What is "good" in one primitive tribe is "bad" in another. They bid us therefore recognize the relativity of all such judgments and then, in the light of our understanding, divest ourselves of the "prejudices" of our own culture.

What they fail to notice is the most striking fact of all: that no enduring society ever has been "unprejudiced" in that sense. Even if they insist upon denying what is here maintained—namely, that to have "prejudices" is a necessary consequence of the nature of man—they should at least admit that such "prejudices" obviously have a tremendous "survival value."

A current college textbook of psychology gives a conveniently simple statement of the relativist position. "Moral conduct," so it says, "is conduct of which a given society approves," and by the absoluteness of its statement it clearly implies that "moral conduct" is also "nothing but" just that. If the author is convinced that this is a truth which it is his duty as a scientist to promulgate, he should at least add also the simple warning: "Undeniable as this fact is, no society which limited itself to this definition has ever endured for long." To try to live without "moral prejudices" (i.e., without making value judgments) is to try to live in a condition so fundamentally repugnant to our nature that it cannot long continue.

Unless we admit that man is a creature to whom moral judgments are "natural," we cannot ask a great many meaningful questions such as, for example, what is the good life, as distinguished from a "high standard of living." We cannot ask them because they can be asked only in connection with some conviction concerning what kind of life it is in the nature of man to lead. And it is because we cannot discuss the good life that it has not become either so unqualified or so accessible as our mastery of the physical environment should make it.

We can ask what are the "needs of industry." We can debate the relative merits of laissez faire, socialism, and any economic system in between—but only so long as we confine ourselves to the question which of them most successfully promotes abundant production, not which makes a good life most accessible. We can also ask what laws and what system of education best meet the needs of either technology or pure science. But we cannot ask *what would best meet the needs of man* or consider the question whether or not, in any specific instance, the "needs of industry" (or even the needs of science) may require some modification in the interests of the possibly conflicting needs of man. We cannot ask any such questions because we have ceased to believe that man has any nature and believe instead that, since he has no needs of his own, he will "adapt" or "adjust" to whatever conditions are most favorable to industry, technology or science, or what not.

The only categorical imperative we accept, almost the only inescapable obligation we feel, is the obligation to realize all the potentialities inherent in technology. Whenever the possibility of moving faster, of producing more, or of exercising any increased power presents itself we accept the duty of moving faster and of wielding more power. What can be done must be done. But we feel no such responsibility toward the potentialities of human nature and we cannot do so as long as we continue to assume that such potentialities do not exist except in so far as they consist in an almost limitless adaptability to the conditions which the nonhuman can create.

That eighteenth century which believed so confidently in the law of nature and appealed so frequently to it fell often into a folly the opposite of ours. Instead of denying that the "natural" or "normal" had any meaning, it was very ready to proclaim that almost any attitude or custom with which it was thoroughly familiar and sympathetic was "in accord with nature" and any conflicting attitude or custom "contrary to nature." It was insufficiently aware—as we certainly are not—that to distinguish between the natural and the merely customary is often extremely difficult, perhaps sometimes impossible.

Against their sometimes fatuous pronouncements "cultural relativism" is in part a protest. Yet the difficulty was never really forgotten even when the reality of the distinction was most unquestioningly accepted. That habit is "second nature" is an idea so old that it fills our literature and John Donne can refer to "that demi-nature custom" without implying that custom is more than a simulacrum. Most certainly it behooves those of us who undertake to assert again that man does have a nature to be fully aware of the difficulties. The nature of man is something which may be inferred, not directly demonstrated, and the more specific any alleged characteristic of that nature is, the less certain it will be that it actually is "nature" and not what Donne called "demi."

We must begin with the minimum assertion that human nature, though enormously variable and exceedingly plastic, is not infinitely so; that though men readily believe and want and do a great variety of different things, they are not readily or very often conditioned to believe or want or do certain others; and that though the discoverable traits of their nature can generally be described only in very general terms our history is sufficiently well known to support the inference that some of the generalities can be stated.

One such probably permanent characteristic of the nature of man has already been mentioned: namely, the persistence with which he makes value judgments of some kind and thus persistently raises the very questions which relativists dismiss as either demonstrably unanswerable or radically meaningless. He insists upon believing that right and wrong are real, that justice and injustice do exist, even though he is not certain what any of them are.

Even if we could get no further than that, we would have already gone a long way. We would have demonstrated that "cultural and moral relativism" is a doctrine repugnant to the nature of man and that the attempt to build a society upon such relativism is certain to reduce him to a condition which he can come to accept comfortably only in so far as he succeeds in dehumanizing himself. Anxiety, tension, and the other forms of malaise whose prevalence so many have observed with alarm are in part the penalty paid by those who have not been completely conditioned into accepting comfortably their condition. The mass-man is the creature who has to some extent escaped the malaise by ceasing to be a man at all.

About the nature of man we shall perhaps never have much detailed knowledge. The very fact that habit can imitate nature so cunningly may forever prevent the development of any body of positive, detailed knowledge comparable to that which has accumulated around other subjects in themselves less important. Perhaps there can never be a real science of man, however much those who are trying to dehumanize him may believe that they have already founded it. The objectivity of science is possible only because it does involve a subject (man) and an object (the external world). But a science of man proposes that the subject—call him the observer, if you like—should be also the object; and that is impossible. Man can observe other men "objectively" only in so far as he excludes from his observation the fact that they are men like himself. Therefore what is nowadays called the science of man is, in actual fact, only the science of man-considered-as-something-less-than-man.

We shall never see ourselves other than through a glass, darkly. For that and for other reasons there will always be disputes over the question whether or not some specific law or custom is or is not "in accord with nature." But to say that is to say only that right and wrong or the beautiful and the ugly must continue to be, as they have always been, to some degree outside the scope of positive knowledge. Yet no matter how inconclusive any discussion which involves them may be, the very fact that the discussion does take place is sufficient to set any society which takes the discussion seriously significantly apart from any society which tends, as our own does, to consider it not worth engaging in. No disagreement concerning *what* is right or wrong is so fundamental as that between those who believe that *some* value judgment is valid and those who believe that none is more valid than any other. Similarly, on a lower level, no two societies can differ so greatly because of what they consider "good manners" as either differs from a society in which no such thing as "good manners" exists.

The appeal to nature will, then, never settle the dispute between the big-endians and the little-endians in any Lilliput. Perhaps, for instance, monogamy is not "natural" and polygamy "unnatural," any more than burial of the dead is the one and cremation the other. But again it may well be true nevertheless that it is "natural" to accept *some* code rather than none at all governing the relations of the sexes —just as it is natural to feel that some ceremonial disposition of the dead is "right and proper."

Should we, however, ever come again to believe that the question whether or not something is "in accord with human nature" is a meaningful—perhaps the most meaningful— question, we shall want to explore this permanent human nature in many directions and test the extent to which it is possible to determine, with some degree of probability at least, characteristics of that nature somewhat more specific than

any so far suggested. Are there any which seem pretty obvious in the light of what we already know about the histories
of cultures?

I myself should confidently say, "Yes, at least one other";
and it is this: Man is not by nature a pure materialist or
satisfied with what are called common-sense value judgments. One of the most evident constants of human nature
is the desire for Goods other than the material, and the vast
majority of cultures have put something else first. They have
sought God as the ancient Hebrews did, or, like the Greeks,
beauty and wisdom. Below those levels they have sometimes
put the highest value on glory, courage, personal prowess, or
military success and believed that comfort as well as security
were well sacrificed for them. Even the belief that a large
collection of shrunken human heads is the thing most to be
desired testifies to the fact that to believe something more
worth having than material wealth is as nearly universal as
the belief that some things are good and some evil. A society
which, like ours, defines the good life as identical with the
high standard of living is running contrary to a fundamental
characteristic of the nature of man.

In *Notes from Underground*, Dostoevsky asked: "Does not
man, perhaps, love something besides well-being?" and then
he half-answered his own question with, "Perhaps he is just as
fond of suffering." This answer is no doubt an exaggeration
—even what we are fond of calling a "neurotic exaggeration."
But perhaps it is only an overstatement of the true reply.
Perhaps the animals do not desire anything except well-
being. That we cannot know. But that man does desire something else is part of his humanity. Call it perversity or call

it the determination to transcend the most obvious Goods. In either case it exists and is important, so important that we might well hesitate before trying to "condition" him out of it. Should we succeed, we might find that we had turned man back into an animal again.

Could we at this moment get no further than the two statements already made, namely, that man is (1) inveterately a maker of value judgments and (2) not by nature a pure materialist or utilitarian, we should already have called attention to the fact that in at least these two important respects the present condition of man is one to which he cannot "adjust" without violating his nature.

Thus the ideal of the welfare state has its dangers unless we are willing to raise seriously the question, "In what does total welfare for a human being consist?" And that question cannot very well be raised without some concept of "normality." Why could we not follow the lead of Shaw's oculist and recognize that the criterion should be what an eye (or a man) *can be* rather than what either most often is? By any such definition a "normal human being" is some kind of individual, while the "average human being" is little more than a mass-man. Today we are obsessed with origins and must stretch a point to consider even potentialties. Perhaps we shall have again to recognize the meaning of entelechy— to ask, that is to say, not merely what was the origin but also what is the destiny of man; not merely what is he but what is he striving to become?

From the two statements already made about normal human nature one might well proceed to raise at least two questions—not to be answered confidently, but upon which would in turn depend the answer to the question whether or not, in two other respects, our society is organized upon "unnatural" assumptions.

Do men naturally desire justice as well as believe that it is a reality? The ancient philosophers thought they did, whereas we moderns have decided that what they desire is only their individual or their class interest instead. Should it turn out that the ancients were even partly right, that might make a great difference in our way of dealing with our fellows—beginning even in the nursery and the kindergarten.

Some child psychologists insist that what children need is "uncritical love" and that they should be made to feel that they can count upon it no matter how "naughty" they may be. Yet it is a common observation that what the unsympathetic call "spoiled" children seem very often extremely unhappy. Can that be because the expectation—the desire, even—that acts should have consequences and that the way one is treated should depend to some extent upon the way one behaves is latent on the not quite blank slate and constitutes the most primitive form of that idea of justice which, in some way and to some extent, all "normal" men do love. Perhaps a world which violently disappoints this expectation is seriously disturbing even to a child. Perhaps the best way to deal with delinquency and crime would be not to assume as we now tend to do that "society" is wholly to blame, but to mix some justice with "understanding." Perhaps if we did so both the delinquent and the criminal would be less "mixed up" just because he found himself in a society which, to that extent, met one of the expectations of normal human nature.

The second question would be whether the technology

which has made the environment of most men who live in every "developed" country one almost wholly man-made has not placed them in what seems to fundamental human nature an abnormal environment. Perhaps the natural context for the human being is the context of the natural world. Once he was surrounded by other living things and his most intimate relations were with other men, with animals, and with plants. Now his most usual and intimate business is with machines. Does that tend to make him machinelike? Is it ultimately responsible for the fact that he has become a mechanist as well as a materialist and thus tries to believe things contrary to his nature?

Both the behavior of man and the condition of man have been exhaustively investigated in our century. Any attempt to investigate his nature would certainly involve such questions as those we have just been raising and they cannot be answered so easily as questions concerning his condition (What proportion of homes has a telephone?) or his behavior (What is the average number of hours he spends in watching television?). But they are more significant. The attempt to study the nature of man would involve both what, on the evidence of history and anthropology, seem to be the constants and perhaps also an attempt to apply that reason which, as Professor Strauss pointed out, may be more important than "common consent" in any successful attempt to discover what "the natural" really is.

Neither method will be easy for us to apply. The first will not be easy because of the inherent difficulty in distinguishing between the habitual and the natural; the second because it must assume the validity of reason despite the fact that of all the faiths which modern man has lost the most disastrous may well be his loss of faith in reason itself. When the eighteenth century ceased to believe in revelation it proclaimed its faith in reason. We dismiss reason as no more than the rationalization of individual interests, class interests, and the prejudices of a particular culture. Unless the lost faith is to some degree recovered no true humanism is possible.

But do we, many will surely ask, dare embark seriously upon any such difficult, even dubious, enterprise? Has it not already been admitted that only when all such enterprises had been abandoned and Western Europe had turned its attention to no questions except answerable questions addressed to external nature, did progress begin? To return again to questions of another sort might jeopardize our technological civilization and open the way to all the gossamer nonsense of metaphysics, the miasma of superstition, and the opiate of dogma.

Such an objection might have been easy to defend no more than a few generations ago, when it was assumed on what seemed to be a solid base of experience that the new world of increasing comfort would continue indefinitely and when, therefore, inner confidence accompanied outward prosperity. But the world, while continuing to grow richer and more powerful, is now restless and apprehensive within. The Age of Confidence has, as no one denies, given way to the Age of Anxiety. The richest and most powerful civilization which ever existed is also the most frightened.

There must be some explanation of this paradoxical situation. If it is not that an exclusive concern with wealth and power do not lead to peace, plenty, and happiness, then what is it? If we have achieved what we thought we most wanted to achieve only to find ourselves threatened by extinction as well as plagued by less concrete anxieties and fears, what explanation is more reasonable than the assumption that what we thought we wanted was not what, or was at least not all, we actually do want? And if that is, indeed, the answer, then what decision could be more reasonable than the decision to ask again, and as searchingly as possible, what we *do* want, what it is in our nature to want and to be satisfied with? If we refuse to ask such questions is there any conceivable program other than that to which, explicitly or implicitly, we are actually committed—namely, the program which aims principally to achieve still more wealth and still more power?

Those who deny that our program is merely this, point out that it includes also a more equitable distribution of the wealth and a wiser use of the power. Thus they try to make the great issue of our time a political issue. But the conflict between those who call themselves democrats and those who advocate one or another variety of totalitarianism is not actually as fundamental as is usually assumed. It is hardly more than a dispute about (a) the method to be followed in achieving similar ends and (b) the rigidity and consistency with which various general assumptions should be insisted upon.

In their most familiar forms, communism, socialism, and liberal capitalism all tend to assume that wealth and power (in one way or another achieved, distributed, and controlled) are both the *sine qua non* of a good society and also the only things necessary, since all other goods (in so far as there are any) may be trusted to emerge spontaneously from them. All three either dogmatically assert or tend to assume also that since society makes men, human nature is whatever a given society makes it.

Because society is organized on these assumptions, man is becoming the mere tender of those machines which he believes are serving him so well. But as he more and more completely submits himself to their needs, as he stands on the production line, drives his car along endless miles of concrete highway, or even guides his jet at speeds beyond the speed of sound, there lie at the back of his mind the nagging questions, "Is this the thing for which I, with my sense of beauty, my passion for justice, my desire to create, and my gift for contemplation was born? What has become of that opportunity to become more fully human which 'the control of nature' was to provide? At what moment did things climb into the saddle and begin to ride me? Am I doomed henceforth to be ridden; or could I somehow once again *use* rather than *be used by* the things which I once hoped to command? I have subjected all living creatures to my will. What is this mere *thing* which is mastering me in its turn? Am I the lord of all creations except of my own? Do all these questions arise because I know everything except myself? Would they be answered if I knew as much about what I am as I know about what I can do?"

Our prophets often describe the "new world" which lies just ahead when atomic power has been harnessed to peaceful uses; when we can travel across space instead of merely through air; or even when the work week has been reduced to twenty-five hours. But there is in actual fact nothing really *new* about this new world. It would be merely one which had taken another step in the direction which many previous steps had taken. New worlds never were and never will be created except by new ideas, or aims, or desires, or convictions. Christianity created a new world and so did the seventeenth century's new faith that a knowledge of the laws of nature could change rapidly and radically mankind's condition. To some slight extent our own age is still part of the new world Christianity created and it is still very much part of the new world which faith in science created. But there will be no newer world as long as there is no idea or ideal newer than that of the seventeenth century?

If we should ever decide that we do want a new world we shall have to find first the faith which could make it. As long as we believe that the only human reality is the human condition there will be no fundamental change in that condition. If we should become convinced again that man has a nature and that the greatest of his needs is to create a condition suited to it, then a really new world might come gradually into being.

Because of their fundamental similarities, liberal capitalism, socialism, and communism are alike in the questions they can and the questions they cannot ask. All three can, for example, ask what system of production and distribution is the most equitable and efficient; none can ask clearly whether or not there is any difference between the good life and a high standard of living. All can ask, "How shall we feed an ever increasing population?" but not, "Is an ever increasing population desirable from the standpoint of human nature itself?"; how the mechanization of life may be still further developed, not whether it is desirable to have a world in which man's contacts are nearly all with brick, concrete, and the machine, rarely if ever with that world of living things of which he is actually a part, though he is being progressively alienated from them until, by now, he is much more likely to think of himself as a kind of machine than as a kind of animal.

None can effectively ask such questions and none can even recognize them as real except in so far as he permits himself the inconsistency of vaguely acknowledging the legitimacy of the assumption that the measurable alone is real, that "average" is not the same as "normal," and that the condition of man is not the same thing as the nature of man.

Unless those truths are recognized, the future condition of man (assuming that he has a future) can only be one of two possible conditions. Either he will continue to be anxious, unhappy, and alienated no matter how rich and how powerful he may have become, or those lines, now still faintly sketched upon the not quite blank slate of his mind, will be at last completely "o'erlaid"—in which case he will have lost what Mr. Oppenheimer has so simply and forcefully called "his humanity." "Conditioning" will have triumphed over "nature" and man will have become in actual fact what so many are insisting that he is and has always been.

Should we, on the other hand, come to believe again that it is legitimate to assume that human nature and the human condition are not necessarily identical and the first not necessarily what the second tends to make it seem, then we could cease to concern ourselves exclusively with what men *can do* and with what they *can be made to be*. We could concern ourselves again with what they *are* and with what they *ought to be*. And having done that we might, even, radically improve a condition which the current philosophy promises only to intensify. "Give me a fulcrum for my lever and I can move the world." But it is just the limitation of all relativisms that they provide no point outside the thing to be moved upon which a lever might rest.

Reviewing two new "serious novels" *Time* magazine (Oct. 13, 1958) began: "From Cervantes to Hemingway, storytellers have assumed that man has hopes and aspirations, and that they could be expressed meaningfully. Bosh, says the new school. Man is a blob, creeping and leaping about a world he cannot control, his words meaningless or hypocritical or both. The best thing a novelist can do, the argument runs, is to ditch the novel as it is now known and write a new kind that shows man as the pitiable blob he is."

If this is no exaggerated description of what a few of the most "advanced" of contemporary novelists and playwrights profess to think of man and no more than a recognizable exaggeration of what many less advanced seem inclined to suggest, then one thing is certain. We will not be rescued by those who believe that normal means only average, that the good life means nothing more than a high standard of living, that moral and immoral are merely the rationalized prejudices of a given society, and that, as a writer in the *American Scholar* recently and roundly proclaimed: "Good and evil are but subjective reflections of the objective organization that technology compels."

·XI·

A Meaning for "Humanism"

"Humanism" has been used to mean too many things to be a very satisfactory term. Nevertheless, and in the absence of a better word, I shall use it here to stand for the complex of attitudes which this discussion has undertaken to defend.

In this sense a humanist is anyone who rejects the attempt to describe or account for man wholly on the basis of physics, chemistry, and animal behavior. He is anyone who believes that will, reason, and purpose are real and significant; that value and justice are aspects of a reality called good and evil and rest upon some foundation other than custom; that consciousness is so far from being a mere epiphenomenon that it is the most tremendous of actualities; that the unmeasurable may be significant; or, to sum it all up, that those human realities which sometimes seem to exist only in the human mind are the perceptions, rather than merely the creations, of that mind. He is, in other words, anyone who says that there are more things in heaven and earth than are dreamed of in the positivist philosophy.

Originally, to be sure, the term humanist meant simply anyone who made the study of ancient literature his chief concern. Obviously it means, as I use it, very much more. But there remains nevertheless a certain connection between the aboriginal meaning and that which I am attempting to give it, because those whom I describe as humanists usually recognize that literature and the arts have been pretty consistently "on their side" and because it is often to literature that they turn to renew their faith in the whole class of truths which the modern world has so consistently tended to dismiss as the mere figments of a wishfully thinking imagination.

In so far as this modern world gives less and less attention to its literary past, in so far as it dismisses that past as something outgrown and to be discarded much as the imperfect technology contemporary with it has been discarded, just to that extent does it facilitate the surrender of humanism to technology. In literature is to be found, directly expressed or, more often, indirectly implied, the most effective correction to the views now most prevalent among the thinking and unthinking alike.

The great imaginative writers present a picture of human nature and of human life which carries conviction and thus gives the lie to all attempts to reduce man to a mechanism. Novels, and poems, and dramas are so persistently concerned with the values which relativism rejects that one might even define literature as the attempt to pass value judgments upon representations of human life. More often than not those of its imagined persons who fail to achieve power and wealth are more successful than those who do not—by standards which the imaginative writer persuades us to accept as valid. And because we do recognize in their re-creations our own sense of what life is like but do not recognize it in the best documented accounts of most biologists, sociologists, political scientists, or psychologists, those of us who are humanists believe the accounts of the poets, novelists, and playwrights to be truer. Literature has been chiefly concerned with the good life as something not identical with the high standard of living and with man as the maker of his destiny rather than as a creature wholly made rather than making. Literature, more than anything else, has kept alive whatever resistance still exists to the various dismal sciences which have come so near to complete triumph everywhere else.

It is no doubt because many people dimly recognize this fact that some "defense of the humanities" has become an expected part of the college commencement address and other formal discussions of the state of the world. But it is because the recognition is wavering and dim that such defenses are commonly so weak and so often take the form of a mere parenthetical remark likely to come down to something like this: "And of course the humanities are important too but I have not time to say more on that subject now." Most of even those who undertake to "defend the humanities" at some length seem often embarrassed by what strikes them as the weakness of their case and to be expressing a sentimental nostalgia for a lost cause rather than faith in a living reality.

What they most usually seem to be saying is that though, of course, it is by science and technology that men *live*, the arts can be expected to furnish certain graces and to provide an opportunity for refined relaxation. Letters and the other arts are, therefore, merely the ornaments of civilized life. But are they not rather, for an age which has little contact with either theology or philosophy, almost the only preservers of what Mr. Oppenheimer calls man's "humanity"?

Listen for a moment to a voice from another age:

"The truth is that knowledge of external nature, and the sciences which that knowledge requires or includes, are not the great or the frequent business of the human mind. Whether we provide for action or conversation, whether we wish to be useful or pleasing, the first requisite is the religious and moral knowledge of right and wrong, the next is an acquaintance with the history of mankind, and with those examples which may be said to embody truth, and prove by events the reasonableness of opinions. Prudence and Justice are virtues and excellences of all times and of all places; we are perpetually moralists, but we are geometricians only by chance."

When Samuel Johnson wrote that passage he was defending what was already beginning to look like a lost cause. To a certain small number of his contemporaries it was, perhaps, still only a powerfully clear statement of an obvious truth. To many others it was a reminder of something men were beginning to forget. But I doubt if there were any to whom it seemed the mere paradox it has by now become. Today the vast majority of thinking men assume without argument that "knowledge of external nature" *is* the great, the frequent, and almost the only legitimate business of men. It is, they think, upon such knowledge of external nature that both our safety and that prosperity by which we set so much store depend. We are not perpetually moralists, and geometricians only by chance. We have become geometricians perpetually and moralists only by chance—if at all.

Moreover, to have become geometricians perpetually we have been led to deny most of Johnson's other fundamental assertions. We may, to be sure, occasionally remember that an acquaintance with the history of mankind is sometimes useful. But even that is useful chiefly to remind us of the follies we should avoid. And even partial agreement stops there. The dominant schools of psychology and sociology are so far from believing that Prudence and Justice are virtues of all times and of all places that they call upon the dominant school of anthropology to support their contention that *nothing* is true of all times and all places and that Prudence and Justice are so far from being the same everywhere that they do not exist except as abstractions derived from the local and temporary customs prevailing at some time and place. Morals are merely mores. There are cultures but no such thing as culture. There are justices, but no such thing as Justice. We are not merely geometers; we are non-Euclidean geometers to whom one premise is as valid as another and there is no truth except what is logically deducible from one arbitrary premise or another.

The most obvious result of the decision made some two centuries or more ago to consider the knowledge of external nature the greatest, the most frequent, and perhaps the exclusive business of the human mind is the physical world in which we live. Had we not made that decision, we should not produce such an abundance of goods, travel so fast, be able to speak across so many miles to such vast hordes of listeners, or, of course, be in a position to destroy so quickly and so easily whole cities full of our fellow human beings.

The second most obvious result is that loss of which I have just spoken, the loss of confidence in any criteria by which the right and the wrong or even the ugly and the beautiful may be distinguished. That we are the better for this loss of what they insist was a misplaced confidence, many positivists are ready to assert. But it is not certain that a good many of the perplexities, the uncertainties, the anxieties, and the dangers which do perplex this present world—despite the fact that it is so much more abundant and powerful than any previous world—are not related to just this loss.

If man has no true nature as distinguished from what his condition at a given time creates; if no persisting needs, tastes, preferences, and capacities are either met or frustrated by that condition; then there is no reason why he should not be as contentedly "adjusted" to the condition of what Johnson calls a "geometrician" exclusively. But if there *is* such a thing as human nature, and if both man's history and his literature give some clue as to what that nature is; if, indeed, they reveal it more surely than all the polls, questionnaires and tests which "geometry" has been able to devise; then Johnson may be right when he suggests that it is in man's nature to be moral and, perhaps, even religious; that it is, as a matter of fact, in accord with his nature to be a moralist perpetually and a geometer only by chance. And if you do believe this to be true, then it may also seem that the deepest cause of the anxiety which has given its name to our age; that the deepest cause of the fact that man is not so secure, so happy, and so content in his age of power and abundance as it would seem that he should be; that he is, indeed, so frequently forced to seek the aid of psychiatrists or those who can minister to a mind diseased that we are told it is impossible to train as many such ministers as are now needed—if all this is true then, it may be, I say, that the deepest reason is simply this: Man's condition as geometer and as the child of geometry is not harmonious with his nature.

However that may be, we are at least coming to realize more and more vividly something which the earliest proponents of salvation by geometry never suspected, namely, that science is not only the solver of problems but also, at the same time, the creator of other problems. That this is to some extent true, we began to realize a long time ago. We realized, for instance, that the invention of the steam engine created the problem of child slavery in factories. We are also beginning to realize that science creates both abundance and the new problem created by the necessity for endlessly increasing consumption—indeed, for increasing sheer waste—if we are not to be buried and smothered under the load of abundance. And, of course, no other such realization ever came with the dramatic suddenness and the terrifying urgency of the realization that when the secret of atomic fission was discovered we were faced with a problem incomparably more threatening than any which science or technology had previously created.

How is that problem to be solved or even to be approached? The usual answer to such a question when it is asked of relatively minor problems has been: With a hair of the dog that bit you. The answer to the problems created by science is more science.

But does past history suggest that this is how the problems

have been solved—when they have been solved at all? In so far as, say, the problem of child slavery was solved, it was not solved by science but by the conscience of mankind. It was man the moralist, not man the geometer, who solved it. It seems indubitably evident that the problem created by atomic fission cannot be solved by more knowledge of the kind which makes atomic fission possible. We come up against the fact, so often asserted and so often unconvincingly denied, that science can tell us *how to do* many different things but not whether any specific thing which *can be done, ought to be done*. It can tell us how to make a uranium bomb and how to make a hydrogen bomb. It can tell how a city full of people may most efficiently, and even most cheaply, be destroyed. But it cannot tell us what city, if any, *ought* to be so destroyed.

Some answer to that question will have to be given. It was given once, more than a decade ago, over Hiroshima. It seems likely enough that we shall have to give an answer again in the possibly not distant future. Whether we did and whether we will again answer it wisely, I will not attempt to say. But one thing is certain. The answer we did give and the answer we will give is not a scientific answer. It was and it will be an answer which depends, not on how man is functioning as a geometer, but on how he is functioning as a moralist.

If morals are nothing but mores, then the answer we will give will depend simply on what deductions are made from the prevailing mores and it will be wise or foolish only to the extent that it is logically consistent with those prevailing mores. But if morals are more than mores; if they are, as Johnson assumed, permanent; and if good morals are defined in terms of what is harmonious with something enduring in man's nature—then the wisdom or folly, the righteousness or the wickedness of the answer will depend upon the extent to which we have a true understanding of man's nature and upon our ability and willingness to act in accordance with it.

Most of even those relativists who are quite convinced that morals are, indeed, nothing but mores, that there is no justice but only conceptions of justice, are ready to grant that the songs and sayings, the folkways and the literature of any people are among the great crystallizers and transmitters of mores and of conceptions of justice. In other words and to be quite specific, it is not science but humanism which will give the answer to the question, "Upon whom and under what conditions shall a city full of human beings be wiped out?"

Probably those who finally formulate and implement the decision will be dimly if at all aware of the ultimate determinants of that decision. Consciously they may well be geometers only, but unconsciously they will be moralists also, because though men may philosophize and moralize well or ill, consciously or unconsciously, philosophize and moralize they must and do. In a civilization like ours, in which only geometry is much regarded, in which the answers that every man must give to moral and aesthetic and metaphysical questions are usually given thoughtlessly and impromptu, most people philosophize badly.

Under these circumstances it is exceedingly odd that those who set out at college commencements and elsewhere to "defend the humanities" should so often seem hard put to find anything very convincing to say; are so prone to speak of mere graces, and to speak in such merely nostalgic—sometimes indeed merely sentimental—terms. "The humanities" are *not* the ornaments of civilization; they are its salvation—if indeed it is to be saved. They are the best embodiments of the most important aspect of that history of mankind which, as Johnson proclaimed, provides us with "those examples which may be said to embody truth and prove by events the reasonableness of opinions." And even if there is no Truth, no Right, no Wrong, and no Justice, then, at least, arts and letters are in any society the principal source of those illusions concerning Truth, Right, Wrong, and Justice which guide its conduct.

Is there any sign, any hope that we will realize in time that we are perpetually compelled to make moral choices as well as to perform certain acts, and that neither technology nor the relativist philosophy can help us to make those choices except at random and without realizing that they are inescapable?

Many of our leading scientists are saying that we are devoting too little time to "fundamental research." We are, they say, using up in technological development our present stock of potentially useful knowledge and are not learning enough of that pure science which is pursued for its own sake though it so often turns out to be unexpectedly useful. No doubt they are right. But we ought to be doing more "fundamental thinking" as well as more fundamental research, devoting more time to those large general questions which the boastfully practical generally regard as mere cobweb spinning. In the long run nothing which any pure scientist can add to our knowledge of the atom might have as much effect upon our future as what some philosopher or even some poet may say. We have used up or cast aside our fundamental thinking.

The delusion of power is like the delusion of wealth. The individual thinks that if only he had more money, all would be well. Nations—indeed, mankind as a whole—believe that they lack nothing except more power. If we could only travel faster, build larger machines, and create more destructive explosions we should achieve an even higher standard of living—and no other good is definable. Throughout the ages moralists have—with little effect, however—attempted at least to expose the delusions associated with the desire for individual wealth. Even today some continue to do so. But few are aware that the pursuit of power is also a kind of folly, and many hail even the atom bomb as merely an unfortunate preliminary to those "peaceful uses of atomic power" which will, at last, usher in that Golden Age which none of our other assumptions of power were quite sufficient to create.

In Samuel Johnson's *Rasselas* the inventor of a flying machine refuses to demonstrate his invention because, so he says, men should not be allowed to fly until they have become virtuous. However unassailable his logic may seem, it is hardly worthwhile to suggest that we should simply agree not to develop any new instruments of power until we know just how good use could be made of them. Neither scientists nor inventors would be likely to accept any such general principle. Neither can mere laws or "plans" bring technology under control. If anything could control it, that would be some change in man himself, who will continue to pursue power rather than wisdom just so long as it is in power that he takes the greatest pride. If his heart were elsewhere then he might—just possibly—accomplish things more worth accomplishing than those with which he is now so busy. He might then follow the logic of his own evolving nature rather than the logic of evolving technology. The tail might then stop wagging the dog.

In a recent book, J. Robert Oppenheimer said: "In some sort of crude sense which no vulgarity, no humor, no overstatement can quite extinguish the physicists have known sin; and this is a knowledge they cannot lose." But what is this sin? Most of those who acknowledge it would answer correctly enough that it has something to do with the invention of the bomb and its use. But is it obviously wrong to beat to the draw an enemy who is trying to destroy you? Only the most uncompromising preachers of nonresistance as an unqualified obligation will say so.

Even more assuredly it is no sin to be a physicist. But if there is a sin of which the physicists were guilty, it was a sin they share with all who follow the faith of our times. It is the sin of believing that *the nature of the atom* is more important than *the nature of man;* that knowledge of matter is more useful, more important, and more significant than knowledge of another kind; that the most valid of injunctions is not "Know thyself" but "Know the Not-Self"; that the key to wisdom is not self-mastery but the mastery of the powers which lie outside of man.

We cannot now "control the machine" because we are hypnotized by it; because we do not really want to control it. And we do not want to control it because in our hearts we believe it more interesting, more wonderful, more admirable, and more rich in potentialities than we ourselves are. We cannot break the hypnosis, cannot wake from our submissive dream, without retracing one by one the steps which brought us more and more completely under its spell.

Those steps were not taken yesterday and they cannot be retraced unless we are both willing and able to reassess the values which the hypnosis has imposed upon us. That would involve a willingness to ask how many of the "advantages" which power has conferred upon us really are advantageous. It would mean also getting rid of all our love of the machine for its own sake, of our delight in the small gadget as well as in the great. But if we did do all that these things imply, then we might begin to recover from our hypnosis.

If there are any signs of such an awakening they are faint and dubious. The main current tends to run in the long-familiar direction. To the average citizen knowledge means science, science means technology, and (a last debasement) the meaning of technology is reduced to "know-how." It took a Russian satellite in the sky to shake our complacency and it was shaken only because it suggested that the Russians had more "know-how" than we. And the lesson most commonly drawn has been that education should put even greater stress upon the development of such know-how, leaving even less time for "fundamental thinking."

Someday we may again discover that "the humanities" are something more than ornaments and graces. Sociology and psychology may again find man's consciousness more interesting than the mechanically determined aspects of his behavior and we may again be more concerned with what man *is* than with *what he has* and *what he can do*. We might again take more pride in his intellect than in his tools; might again think of him as pre-eminently *Homo sapiens* rather than *Homo faber*—man the thinker rather than man the maker. We might—at some distant day—come to realize again that the proper study of mankind is man. ⟨

But that time is certainly not yet. We have forgotten that know-how is a dubious endowment unless it is accompanied by other "knows"—by "know what," "know why," and—most important of all at the present moment—"know whether." Quite blandly and as a matter of course we still ask what are the needs of industry, not what are the needs of man.

In the Sanskrit Panchatantra, that collection of romantic tales written down in an early century A.D., there is a fable which might have been devised for today. Three great magicians who have been friends since boyhood have continued to admit to their fellowship a simple fellow who was also a companion of their youth. When the three set out on a journey to demonstrate to a wider world the greatness of their art they reluctantly permit their humble friend to accompany them, and before they have gone very far, they come upon a pile of bones under a tree. Upon this opportunity to practice their art they eagerly seize. "I," says the first, "can cause these dead bones to reassemble themselves into a skeleton." And at his command they do so. "I," says the second, "can clothe that skeleton with flesh." And his miracle, also, is performed. Then, "I," says the third, "can now endow the whole with life."

At this moment the simpleton interposes. "Don't you realize," he asks, "that this is a tiger?" But the wise men are scornful. Their science is "pure"; it has no concern with such vulgar facts. "Well then," says the simpleton, "wait a moment." And he climbs a tree. A few moments later the tiger is indeed brought to life. He devours the three wise men and

210

departs. Thereupon the simpleton comes down from his tree and goes home.

There is no more perfect parable to illustrate what happens when know-how becomes more important than common sense—and common sense is at least the beginning of wisdom.

The ancients had a wise motto: *"Quo Urania ducit"*—Wherever Wisdom leads. We have somehow mistranslated or perverted it. Our motto has become *"Quo Uranium ducit."* And that, of course, is the antithesis of humanism.

ABOUT THE AUTHOR

JOSEPH WOOD KRUTCH, drama critic, scholar, and essayist, was born in Knoxville, Tennessee, in 1893. After receiving advanced degrees from Columbia University, Dr. Krutch began teaching at his alma mater in 1917. Later he devoted some years primarily to writing and then returned to Columbia as professor of English. In 1943 he became Brander Matthews professor of dramatic literature at the same university. Dr. Krutch was the drama critic of the *Nation* from 1924 until 1950, missing only the two years he spent in Europe on a Guggenheim fellowship.

Since the publication of *The Modern Temper* in 1929, Joseph Wood Krutch has been well known for four kinds of books: his studies of dramatists and the theatre; his works on the eighteenth century, including a biography of Samuel Johnson; his books on nature; and his astute studies of man and society.

Besides his own many books, he has edited the plays of Congreve and O'Neill, the English translation of *Remembrance of Things Past*, and major anthologies on philosophical and social themes.

In 1950 Dr. Krutch retired from teaching, gave up his position on the *Nation*, and moved to Arizona, where he wrote *The Desert Year*, his recorded observations of the desert country. His writings on New England—*Twelve Seasons* and *The Best of Two Worlds* —gave similarly joyful testimony to the delights of nature in another region. *The Measure of Man*, a discussion of the problems of modern man, won the National Book Award for nonfiction in 1955. His most recent books are *The Great Chain of Life* and *Grand Canyon*.

In recent years Dr. Krutch has divided his time between the New England countryside and the Southwest, and, with his wife, now makes his home in Arizona.